OECD Skills Studies

Effective Adult Learning Policies

CHALLENGES AND SOLUTIONS FOR LATIN AMERICAN COUNTRIES

This work is published under the responsibility of the Secretary-General of the OECD. The opinions expressed and arguments employed herein do not necessarily reflect the official views of OECD member countries.

This document, as well as any data and map included herein, are without prejudice to the status of or sovereignty over any territory, to the delimitation of international frontiers and boundaries and to the name of any territory, city or area.

The statistical data for Israel are supplied by and under the responsibility of the relevant Israeli authorities. The use of such data by the OECD is without prejudice to the status of the Golan Heights, East Jerusalem and Israeli settlements in the West Bank under the terms of international law.

Note by Turkey
The information in this document with reference to "Cyprus" relates to the southern part of the Island. There is no single authority representing both Turkish and Greek Cypriot people on the Island. Turkey recognises the Turkish Republic of Northern Cyprus (TRNC). Until a lasting and equitable solution is found within the context of the United Nations, Turkey shall preserve its position concerning the "Cyprus issue".

Note by all the European Union Member States of the OECD and the European Union
The Republic of Cyprus is recognised by all members of the United Nations with the exception of Turkey. The information in this document relates to the area under the effective control of the Government of the Republic of Cyprus.

Please cite this publication as:
OECD (2020), *Effective Adult Learning Policies: Challenges and Solutions for Latin American Countries*, OECD Skills Studies, OECD Publishing, Paris, *https://doi.org/10.1787/f6b6a726-en*.

ISBN 978-92-64-44582-6 (print)
ISBN 978-92-64-46394-3 (pdf)

OECD Skills Studies
ISSN 2307-8723 (print)
ISSN 2307-8731 (online)

Photo credits: Cover © Studio Foltzer - Nakigitsune-sama / Shutterstock.com.

Corrigenda to publications may be found on line at: *www.oecd.org/about/publishing/corrigenda.htm*.
© OECD 2020

The use of this work, whether digital or print, is governed by the Terms and Conditions to be found at *http://www.oecd.org/termsandconditions*.

Foreword

Globalisation and rapid technological change, together with demographic developments are reshaping skill demands and supply in all countries. These trends are expected to continue in the coming years at an increasing pace and to substantially affect Latin America and Caribbean (LAC) countries. Technological change is reshaping people's lives, workplaces and economies, profoundly transforming the world of work and, in turn, the skills demanded by employers.

Skills are crucial to thrive in such increasingly changing landscapes and the extent to which individuals will be able to harness the benefits stemming from technological progress will depend on their ability to maintain relevant skills over their working careers and the preparedness of their country's adult learning system.

This report draws on the new information contained in the OECD Survey of Adult Skills (PIAAC), the Skills for Jobs database as well as other international databases to assess the readiness of LAC countries' adult learning systems to the new and upcoming challenges of the future of work.

In particular, this report identifies the specific megatrends that are reshaping the world of work in LAC countries by looking at the potential disruptive impact that automation and technological change will have on workers and firms in the region. The report also discusses the substantial impact that population ageing and demographic changes will have on adult learning systems and suggests ways to prepare countries and firms to effectively react to these changes.

Several specific challenges emerge. Among those, the report provides an overview of the most salient gaps that affect the inclusiveness of adult learning systems in the Latin America and Caribbean (LAC) region. It also discusses the actions that can be taken to make the access more inclusive and to boost participation of adults in learning activities. The report also provides an assessment of the role of government, employers and individuals in the governance and financing of adult learning. It discusses the limits of existing approaches and provides examples of international best practices to improve the co-ordination and coherence across all actors of the adult learning system.

This report was prepared by Elena Crivellaro from the OECD Centre for Skills, under the supervision of Fabio Manca (Head of the Skills Analysis team). Montserrat Gomendio (Head of the OECD Centre for Skills) and Andrew Bell (Head of the National Skills Strategy project) provided guidance, oversight and comments. Stefano Scarpetta (OECD Director for Employment, Labour and Social Affairs) ensured strategic oversight for the project. The report has benefitted from helpful comments provided by staff at the Banco Santander.

Jennifer Cannon co-ordinated production and provided valuable support in the editorial process, while Rasa Silyte-Niavas provided administrative support.

This report was made possible by a financial contribution from Banco Santander. The views expressed in this report should not be taken to reflect the official position of Banco Santander. This report is published under the responsibility of the Secretary-General of the OECD.

Table of contents

Foreword 3

Executive summary 7

1 Assessment and recommendations 9
    Megatrends are reshaping the world of work and societies 10
    LAC countries have made substantial progress in improving the coverage and the quality of their education systems but challenges remain 11
    Low levels of participation in adult learning are a common challenge across many countries but lack of participation is especially worrisome in LAC countries 11
    Several barriers hinder participation in adult learning, from lack of inclusiveness, financial and time constraints or family obligations 12
    Aligning skill development and adult learning to the demands of the labour market is of fundamental importance 13
    Digitalisation plays a fundamental role in shaping skill demands and countries in the region are already taking some measures to develop relevant skills 13
    All stakeholders, public and private, need to contribute equitably to steering and fostering lifelong learning activities 14

2 Why is adult learning important in Latin America? 17
    Summary of the main results 18
    Factors affecting and reshaping skill demands in Latin America 20
    References 34
    Notes 36

3 Coverage and inclusiveness of adult learning in Latin America 38
    Summary of the main insights 39
    Participation in adult learning 41
    Inclusiveness of adult learning systems in Latin America 44
    Barriers to training participation in Latin America 50
    References 52
    Notes 54

4 Policies to spur adult learning in Latin America: Challenges and solutions 55
    Summary of the main insights 56
    Public provided training in Latin America 59
    Private-sector supported training in Latin America 67
    A coherent approach is needed: The role of a whole-of-stakeholders approach 71
    Effective financial incentives to encourage employers participation in adult learning 74

| References | 78 |
| Notes | 81 |

FIGURES

Figure 2.1. Agriculture and industry sectors make up a large share of employment in LAC	21
Figure 2.2. A large share of jobs are at high risk of automation or significant change	22
Figure 2.3. Job quality in LAC countries is low compared to other OECD countries	25
Figure 2.4. Informality is still pervasive in the LAC region	26
Figure 2.5. Latin America needs to continue to raise educational attainment	27
Figure 2.6. School results and equity remain a challenge	28
Figure 2.7. The proportion of low performers in literacy and numeracy	29
Figure 2.8. Finding the right skills can be difficult in Latin America (Employer reported labour market imbalances)	30
Figure 2.9. Share of employment in high demand, by skills level	32
Figure 2.10. Qualification mismatch is high in Latin America	33
Figure 2.11. Skills shortage indicators for selected LAC and OECD countries	34
Figure 3.1. Adults' participation in learning is insufficient in many countries	42
Figure 3.2. Participation in informal learning	42
Figure 3.3. Training participation of workers with and without a contract	44
Figure 3.4. Gap in participation, by socio-demographic characteristics	45
Figure 3.5. Gap in participation, by wage and employment characteristics	46
Figure 3.6. Perceptions towards training usefulness	50
Figure 3.7. Reasons preventing participation in (more) formal and/or non-formal education	51
Figure 4.1. Spending on active labour market policies is below the OECD average	60
Figure 4.2. Open education in Latin America	66
Figure 4.3. Incidence and intensity of on-the-job training in formal firms in Latin America	68
Figure 4.4. Employers' investment in training could be improved	69
Figure 4.5. SMEs are less likely to provide training to their workers	70
Figure 4.6. Management score, average 2004-2015	71

TABLES

Table 2.1. Old-age dependency ratios: Historical and projected values, 1950-2075	24
Table 2.2. Occupational shortage and surplus in Latin America	33
Table 3.1. Likelihood of training participation, by individual, job and firm characteristics	49
Table 4.1. Characteristics of NTIs	63
Table 4.2. Benefits and drawbacks of training levies and tax incentives for firms	75

Follow OECD Publications on:

http://twitter.com/OECD_Pubs

http://www.facebook.com/OECDPublications

http://www.linkedin.com/groups/OECD-Publications-4645871

http://www.youtube.com/oecdilibrary

http://www.oecd.org/oecddirect/

Executive summary

In Latin America, as across the globe, globalisation and rapid technological change, together with demographic developments are reshaping skill demands and supply in all countries. These trends are expected to continue in the coming years at an increasing pace. Technological progress, in particular, is profoundly transforming the world of work and, in turn, the skills demanded by employers. This poses challenges but it also creates opportunities for Latin American and the Caribbean (LAC) countries in the near future. While many jobs could be "technically automatable", automation may not be yet economically attractive or viable for many firms in LAC economies, as costly investments in advanced technology are usually out of reach to most entrepreneurs, especially for small and medium-sized enterprises (SMEs) in the region. Similarly, labour is still a cheaper option than automation in the region. This leaves room for policy makers in LAC countries to anticipate the potential change and react accordingly.

Forecasts, however, predict that it is only a matter of time before LAC countries will widely adopt new technologies, potentially affecting millions of jobs and workers in the region. As digital technologies gradually spread across the region, online learning offers a significant opportunity to leverage broadband network access to spread knowledge in a cost-effective way. Massive Open Online Courses (MOOCs), academic courses offered online often provided at no cost, aim at large-scale interactive participation from around the world. These, however, face challenges of implementation in the region. Evidence shows that individuals who are more likely to participate in open education in Latin America, as across OECD countries more broadly, are mainly young, educated and skilled workers. This situation potentially leaves out the most vulnerable and the low skilled most in need of receiving training. More effort is needed to strengthen the ICT skills of disadvantaged groups and to create suitable options for them to use digital technologies for learning.

Demographic dynamics have important implications on skills demand and supply. Population ageing is likely to put considerable pressure on education and training systems as it increases the need for individuals to maintain and update their skills over the life-course in the context of longer working lives. In Latin America, a large proportion of the region's population is still young and this creates a demographic dividend. This window of opportunity, however, may be closing soon as the number of young people is expected to fall after 2020.

Against this backdrop, evidence presented in this report highlights how LAC countries need to boost participation in high-quality training and, especially, in adult learning where countries in the region are lagging particularly behind. Participation in adult learning in the region is more than 10 percentage points below the OECD average. Non-participation in adult leaning is particularly worrying. Approximately 57% of adults did not participate – and did not want to participate – in adult learning activities (compared to the OECD average of 49%). In addition, in LAC countries, the incidence of adults' participation in training varies considerably depending on socio-economic backgrounds and/or on the employment status of the individual. The participation of women in learning activities is lower than that of men across the countries in the region.

In Latin America, smaller firms are also less likely to provide training to workers than larger firms. Data from the Survey of Adult Skills (PIAAC) show that only 40% of workers in SMEs participated in training, compared to 69% workers in larger firms. While a similar pattern can be found in all other countries participating and across OECD countries, in Latin America the gap in training provision between small and large firms is almost twice as high as the OECD average.

Boosting the participation of individuals and firms in adult learning calls for a holistic approach and for the recognition that the different actors that are involved in adult learning may respond differently to specific sets of incentives. Failure to engage each actor of the system with targeted interventions can hinder the overall participation and promote an unequal participation in adult learning.

Policy intervention aimed at fostering employers' engagement in training should, for instance, raise awareness about the benefits of training amongst employers and help them identify their own skills needs and potential funding opportunities (i.e. tax incentives, levies or subsidies) that could be leveraged to provide training to their workers.

Policy intervention should also be aimed at building the capacity of employers to provide truly relevant training to their workers and to understand and plan on what skills will be needed in the future. Employers, especially those operating in the small firms in LAC countries, lack the resources to carry out sophisticated workforce planning exercises and to provide training accordingly. Governments, therefore, can act in both cases by supporting and targeting specific firms with subsidies to build skills development capacity and reduce training costs while also strengthening their efficacy.

Finally, policy makers should consider setting up well-designed financial incentives to boost engagement in training, aiming to strike the right balance between the support to firms and individuals, on the one hand, and the prevention of potential deadweight losses, on the other.

1 Assessment and recommendations

This chapter provides an overview of the main challenges faced by the adult learning systems of Latin American and Caribbean (LAC) countries and of the solutions discussed throughout the report. Megatrends such as globalisation or demographic changes are already reshaping skill demands and LAC countries need to reinforce their response by providing tailored policy intervention to boost participation of all individuals in learning, strengthening incentives for low skilled and women to engage in learning and supporting firms and employers in planning talent and skill development accordingly.

Megatrends are reshaping the world of work and societies

In Latin America, as across the globe, globalisation and rapid technological change, together with demographic developments are reshaping skill demands and supply in all countries. These trends are expected to continue in the coming years at an increasing pace. Technological progress, in particular, is profoundly transforming the world of work and, in turn, the skills demanded by employers. This poses challenges but it also creates opportunities for Latin American and the Caribbean (LAC) countries in the near future.

Technological change and automation

Recent OECD estimates suggest that on average across Chile, Ecuador, Mexico and Peru 24% of jobs will face a high risk of automation. This figure is around 9 percentage points higher than the OECD average. An additional 35% of jobs in the region are likely to experience significant changes in the tasks that workers carry out daily, a figure that is approximately 5 percentage points higher than the OECD average. LAC countries are, therefore, exposed to potential disruption. Effective adult learning systems are needed to equip adults with the right skills to face the coming challenges.

That being said, while many jobs could be "technically automatable", automation may not be yet economically attractive or viable for many firms in LAC economies as costly investments in advanced technology are usually out of reach to most entrepreneurs, especially for small and medium-sized enterprises (SMEs) in the region. Similarly, labour is still a cheaper option than automation in the region. This leaves room for policy makers in LAC countries to anticipate the potential change and react accordingly. Countries and employers alike need to act now by reinforcing education and training systems and ensure that individuals develop today the skills that will be needed in the future in growing occupations and sectors.

Demographic change

Demographic dynamics have important implications on skills demand and supply. Population ageing is likely to put considerable pressure on education and training systems as it increases the need for individuals to maintain and update their skills over the life-course in the context of longer working lives.

In Latin America, a large proportion of the region's population is still young and this creates a demographic dividend. This window of opportunity, however, may be closing soon as the number of young people is expected to fall after 2020. Brazil and Chile, for instance, are projected to have a higher old-age dependency ratio than most OECD and G20 countries by 2075. The retirement of large cohorts of adults from the labour market can lead to significant shortages of qualified labour; a gap that can only be filled through the continuous training of the existing workforce and the creation of effective adult learning systems. The participation of older workers in adult learning activities is, nonetheless, very low and LAC countries need to put more effort in supporting these workers who are likely to suffer from changes in skills demands stemming from technological change.

Job quality and informality

Job quality is also a major concern in Latin America, where individuals experience lower average earnings and higher levels of earnings inequality than across OECD countries. Workers in Latin America tend to be more vulnerable than their counterparts in more advanced economies. High and persistent informal employment represents another major policy concern, ranging between 9% in Uruguay to 65% of total employment in Guatemala.

Reinforcing the skills of disadvantaged individuals (most of whom who are low skilled), is key to fight informality and poor job-quality, but workers in those jobs have limited access to training opportunities relative to workers in the formal and high-quality labour market. This situation further exacerbates inequalities.

Evidence shows that in all LAC countries, the probability of being employed in the informal sector decreases dramatically with the level of education of a worker. In Colombia, for instance, recent evidence points to skill upgrading as a major driver of the reduction in informality from 70% in 2007 to 62% in 2017.

The low skills of many LAC employers and in particular, the shortage of educated entrepreneurs in the informal sector, is an important factor driving persistent levels of informality. In Guatemala and Brazil respectively, for instance, only 8% and 13% of managers in the informal sector have a college degree. Poor managerial practices, associated to low skills of many entrepreneurs in the informal sector, are associated with low productivity and, in turn, with scarce resources and incentives to engage in training in those firms. This creates a vicious circle that perpetuates informality, low productivity and insufficient skills accumulation. Supporting the development of good managerial practices and boosting the number of well-educated entrepreneurs could contribute significantly to reduce the number of informal firms by increasing productivity and strengthening engagement in training.

LAC countries have made substantial progress in improving the coverage and the quality of their education systems but challenges remain

Only 64.2% of individuals aged 25-34 years old in the region has completed secondary education. This figure is about 20 percentage points lower than the OECD average (84%). In addition, only 24% of 25-34 year-olds hold a tertiary degree relative to 43% on average across OECD countries. Insufficient skill development in formal education (from primary to tertiary) has scarring effects on the likelihood of adults to participate in further training and, therefore, it represents a barrier for LAC countries to effectively address the challenges of the future of work.

It is not only the quantity of enrolled students, however, but also the relatively poor quality of LAC region's education and training systems that represents a key challenge in many countries. The OECD's Programme for International Student Assessment (PISA) measures 15-year-olds' proficiency in reading, mathematics and science. Across many LAC countries, PISA scores are substantially below the OECD average and that of other emerging economies. Worryingly, the socio-economic background of students plays a prominent role in students' scores in LAC countries, much more than the average across OECD countries.

Progress has been made in the last decade in many LAC countries to ensure that education and training systems are more inclusive and to boost their quality for students of all backgrounds. Many countries, however, are still struggling. For example, in Peru the socio-economic status of students still explains more than 20% of the variation in PISA scores in science. Socio-economic status also plays a great role in Chile, Costa Rica and Colombia where its impact is well above that observed in the average across OECD countries. Furthermore, in Chile and Colombia the importance of socio-economic background in explaining students' performance increased considerably between 2006 and 2015.

Low levels of participation in adult learning are a common challenge across many countries but lack of participation is especially worrisome in LAC countries

Further evidence highlights how LAC countries need to boost participation in high-quality training and, especially, in adult learning where countries in the region are lagging particularly behind. The Survey of Adult Skills, a product of the Programme for the International Assessment of Adult Competencies (PIAAC) shows, in fact, that in many LAC countries (Chile, Ecuador, Mexico and Peru) up to 60% of adults have low levels of skills – both in terms of literacy and numeracy proficiency. This calls for immediate action to boost the participation in up-skilling and learning activities for many adults in the region.

Participation in adult learning in the region is also more than 10 percentage points below the OECD average. Non-participation in adult leaning is particularly worrying. Approximately 57% of adults did not participate – and did not want to participate – in adult learning activities (compared to the OECD average of 49%). However, participation in adult learning is very heterogeneous across countries in the region. Chile and Peru for instance, show levels of participation that are similar to those of some developed economies such as Japan or Spain and even higher than in certain other OECD countries like Greece, Italy and Turkey. Other LAC countries, instead, lag far behind and too many adults are uninterested in participating in training.

The average duration of training is also shorter in Latin America than across OECD countries with the median number of hours spent on non-formal job related learning per year (an indicator of the intensity of the participation) being significantly lower in LAC countries than the OECD average. Furthermore, the type of training differs between LAC countries and OECD countries. In Latin America, adults participate more often in informal and less structured training than their peers in OECD countries. On average, for instance, 80% of workers in LAC countries report to learn by doing or from observing others, keeping their skills up-to-date with new products or services at least once per week but in an informal setting.

Informality influences participation in training and skill development and this link is especially important in Latin America. Informality reduces participation in training activities as informal firms are usually small, and have few resources and incentives to devote to training of their workers. This situation perpetuates a vicious circle where informal workers do not train and their lack of skills leads makes them more likely to find jobs in the informal sector than in the formal sector. Providing flexible, cheaper and more accessible learning options to both employees and employers could reverse this trend, helping individuals building labour market relevant skills and igniting a virtuous circle leading to high-quality and formal jobs.

The Survey of Adults Skills (PIAAC) shows that workers employed without a regular contract are, on average, less than half as likely to participate in learning activities than their peers who are employed formally. In some countries, such as Ecuador, the difference in participation in learning activities between workers with and without an employment contract is staggering: approximately 42 percentage points.

Several barriers hinder participation in adult learning, from lack of inclusiveness, financial and time constraints or family obligations

Providing truly inclusive learning opportunities for all and, particularly, to individuals in a region with high levels of inequality such as Latin America is, therefore, of paramount importance. In LAC countries, however, the incidence of adults' participation in training varies considerably depending on socio-economic backgrounds and/or on the employment status of the individual.

Low skilled individuals, who tend to be in lower-quality jobs and often in the informal economy, participate substantially less in training. One extra year of education is associated with an increase in participation in training of approximately 0.4% across OECD countries and approximately 0.5% in Latin America.

Employment status and job-quality are also strongly related to the take-up of training. According to the Survey of Adult Skills (PIAAC) data, on average in Latin America, the participation rate of the low-wage workers is 26 percentage points lower than that of higher-wage employees. This result is likely to be self-reinforcing, as individuals participating less in training are also those who struggle the most to find high-quality and well-paid jobs.

Gender plays an important role when it comes to participating in training. Across LAC countries, the participation of women in learning activities is lower than that of men. Being a woman reduces the likelihood of participating in job-related training by 8% across OECD countries and by almost 19% in LAC countries. This result is driven by the large gap in participation between men and women in Chile, Ecuador, and Peru. Also, marital status plays a far more important role in LAC countries than across OECD countries and being married reduces the likelihood to participate in training by approximately 17% in LAC countries (while it is not statistically significant across OECD countries).

Perhaps surprisingly, however, workers with dependent children in LAC countries are significantly more likely to participate in job-related training activities than across OECD countries. One possible explanation relates to the existence of numerous social protection training programmes (e.g. *Jovenes* Programmes or those for poor households) that have been implemented in the last two decades and that are targeting vulnerable families in many LAC countries.

Finally, in contrast with the majority of OECD countries, LAC countries display a very small gap in participation in adult learning between the unemployed and the employed population (only 8 percentage point differences vs. 17 percentage points across OECD countries). This result is because most unemployed individuals in LAC countries are young and are also the recipients of most public training programmes for adults.

Aligning skill development and adult learning to the demands of the labour market is of fundamental importance

A large share of employment in LAC economies is found in low to medium-tech sectors such as manufacturing and agriculture. In countries such as Argentina, Brazil, Chile, Mexico or Peru the shortages of highly skilled professionals is significantly lower than the OECD average, with less than 2 out of 10 jobs in shortage being "high-skilled" and the majority of jobs in demand being found in medium to low-skilled occupations in the manufacturing and agriculture sectors.

Occupational and skill shortages are, however, rather heterogeneous across countries and call for tailored policy intervention. In Chile, for instance, labourers in the mining and construction sector have experienced robust wage growth, signalling a strong demand for low-medium skilled workers in the country. At the same time, business and administration professionals have also seen a sharp increase in both their hours worked and wages, implying a sustained demand for these medium-skilled professionals. In Brazil, however, where the largest demand is in middle-skill professionals, health associate professional and personal care workers have been on the rise in recent years, while wages have been declining in traditionally high-skilled occupations such as science and engineering professionals, signalling a decrease in demand. Technical skills are also in strong demand in both Mexico and Chile, while Argentina's shortages are in social as well as in basic and complex problem solving skills. Surpluses of complex problem solving skills are found in Peru where demand for high-level skills is weak. In sum, skill demands are varied within the region and what works in one country may not work in another. Tailored interventions, which rely on robust Skill Assessment and Anticipation (SAA) information, is key to fill skill gaps in the labour market, develop relevant curricula, and ensure that demand and supply of skills match.

Digitalisation plays a fundamental role in shaping skill demands and countries in the region are already taking some measures to develop relevant skills

When considering the impact of new technologies on skill imbalances, evidence shows that digitalisation has been slow in making its way in Latin America. Forecasts, however, predict that it is only a matter of time before LAC countries will adopt these technologies more broadly, potentially affecting millions of jobs and workers in the region.

Governments in Latin America are already designing training interventions to respond to the skill challenges of more connected and digital labour markets. In Mexico, for instance, 32 Digital Inclusion Centres (*Puntos Mexico Conectado – Centros de Inclusión Digital*) have been set up across the country, providing basic digital skills programmes. Peru passed the National Digital Literacy Plan to train individuals in ICT (information and communications technology) skills, the use of computer tools as well as mobile devices. Around 107 online courses were made available also to teachers as part of the *Educate Peru Programme* with emphasis on developing digital skills to incorporate ICT use in the classroom. Costa Rica and Brazil have been devoting resources to finance the development of ICT skills in universities and graduate courses.

As digital technologies gradually spread across the region, online learning offers a significant opportunity to leverage broadband network access to spread knowledge in a cost-effective way. Massive Open Online Courses (MOOCs), academic courses offered online often provided at no cost, aim at large-scale interactive participation from around the world. These, however, face challenges of implementation in the region. Evidence shows that individuals, who are more likely to participate in open education in Latin America, as across OECD countries more broadly, are mainly young, educated and skilled workers. This situation potentially leaves out the most vulnerable and the low skilled most in need of receiving training. More effort is needed to strengthen the ICT skills of disadvantaged groups and to create suitable options for them to use digital technologies for learning.

While the use of new technologies could potentially bring substantial benefits for learning, governments also need to create the framework conditions for all individuals to access those training opportunities. Among the different policy interventions, governments in Latin America need to build data collection infrastructures to support the timely analysis of labour market needs and inform curricula revisions. This is not always easy. SAA exercises do not always respond effectively to the varying needs of different potential policy uses or are insufficiently disaggregated at the regional, sub-regional or sectoral levels for the policy makers to be able to use them.

Some countries in Latin America have implemented good initiatives to improve their labour market and skills information and those can be potentially useful to match skill demand and supply. In Chile, for instance, the Public Employment Service uses information on labour demand, collected through interviews, surveys and roundtables, to align their training offer with labour market needs. In addition, the government runs an online portal called the National Employment Exchange (BNE), a free site where companies publish job offers and workers can submit CVs for consideration. In the Dominican Republic, the Ministry of Labour created a job portal that matches employers with potential workers. In Brazil, as part of the *Pronatec* programme, different ministries can submit requests to the Ministry of Education for creating specific training programmes that correspond to the identified skill needs. The Ministry of Education centralises these requests and co-ordinates the opening of funded training programmes with public and private training providers.

All stakeholders, public and private, need to contribute equitably to steering and fostering lifelong learning activities

On average, the amount spent by LAC countries in active labour market policies (ALMPs) is almost half of that of the OECD average. In addition, wide differences exist between OECD and LAC countries when it comes to the focus, scope and configuration of ALMPs policies. With the exception of Colombia and Chile, public spending for training measures in LAC countries is well below the OECD average. For instance, in Argentina, spending on training is roughly half that of the OECD average, and in Mexico and Brazil, funding allocated to training has decreased considerably in recent years, reaching very low levels.

One traditional way to support training in Latin America has been to subsidise its supply through the creation of National Training Institutes (NTI). NTIs, public agencies in charge of supplying and overseeing Adult Learning funded by the government, are financed with a specific tax on the payroll of formal workers that ranges from 0.25% (Uruguay) to 2% (Colombia). Evidence suggests that even when public investments in NTIs are sizable, the effectiveness of their actions could be strengthened. In particular, the training provided by NTIs reaches only a small fraction of employed workers. In the region, less than 15% of employed workers accessed training provided by NTIs – the only exception is Colombia where up to 24% of workers were involved.

Despite the weak take up of training made available by NTIs, evidence shows that some 30% to 50% of LAC firms in the manufacturing sector still offered training through short, structured courses focusing on specific job-related skills. This signals a substantial direct involvement of employers in supporting training in LAC countries. The OECD Survey of Adult Skills (PIAAC) shows that, on average, across LAC countries, 63% of workers who participated in training report to have received funding from her/his employers for at least one learning activity. Mexico shows the largest share of workers receiving direct support from employers, above 80%. These results, however, only refer to workers in formal firms, and little can be said about the engagement of informal firms in training, these latter representing the majority of businesses in the region.

The average figures discussed above mask great heterogeneity across firms of different sizes, with SMEs engaging in the provision of training activities much less than larger firms in the region. Evidence shows that only 40% of workers in SMEs participated in training, compared to 69% workers in larger firms. While a similar pattern can be found in all other countries participating in the OECD Survey of Adult Skills (PIAAC), in Latin America the gap in training participation between small and large firms is almost twice as large (approx. 30%) as the OECD average (17%). The gap in Ecuador and Mexico is even greater than 30%. This particularly worrying and represents a key challenge for LAC countries, as SMEs account for more than 80% of employment and more than 90% of firms in the region.

Recent evidence for LAC countries shows that an increase in the number of skilled workers in the firm increases productivity, but this result holds only for manufacturing firms with more than 100 employees. A 1% increase in the share of high-skilled workers could lead, on average, to a 0.7% increase in productivity in large firms. No such effect is found in small firms. Part of the difference in the way large and small firms are able to benefit from skilled workers is likely to be explained by the differences in managerial skills across firms of different sizes.

A range of market failures and barriers such as the lack of information, capacity and/or resources means that investment in education and training by employers remains sub-optimal, particularly in the case of SMEs. Creating employer networks can be a solution to the lack of managerial skills and resources in SMEs as these often provide leadership and management skills programmes, in addition to their role as facilitators of knowledge exchange and capacity building. Networks of employers have also the key advantage of pooling the resources of smaller actors together, creating a critical mass and economies of scale that SMEs can leverage to their own advantage.

In addition, other solutions could be used to spur the participation of firms of all sizes in adult learning. Well-designed financial incentives steered by government intervention can be a useful tool to boost incentives to participate in training. There are important caveats however, when designing and implementing financial incentives. As with any policy intervention, a key challenge is, in fact, to ensure the effectiveness of the incentive while minimising potential deadweight losses.

First, the design of financial incentives needs to consider the institutional context as well as the specific objectives that a policy intervention is meant to achieve. In the case of skill development policies, before introducing any intervention the policy maker should carefully assess the reasons for any apparent under-investment in training and the best way to create (or restore) adequate incentives with minimum intervention.

Second, the efficacy of financial incentives depends on a range of framework conditions being in place in the country. For instance, while providing financial support to firms may be desirable to reduce the cost associated to their participation in training, doing so without setting up a solid skills information system that supports employers in making informed decisions on the choice of education providers or on the skills to be developed, may lead to a considerable waste of resources.

Targeting financial incentives at employers rather than at individuals has the advantage that training is more likely to meet the specific needs of the firms and, therefore, to fill concrete gaps in labour market needs. One drawback, however, is that, by providing direct and unconditional support to employers through cash transfers or tax credits, the government risks not being able to reach disadvantaged and vulnerable workers, as employers have weaker incentives to provide training to those groups. Intermediate solutions can be found so that the financial incentives are designed to reach employers under the condition that these provide training also to disadvantaged workers. Funds can also be made conditional on supplying training to the unemployed to ensure their re-inclusion in the labour market and ensure that adult learning plays a key role in ensuring that all citizens develop the skills that will be needed to face the challenges of the future of work. A multipronged approach is needed, where different tools and instruments are used jointly and tailored to the specific policy objective and context of the country.

2 Why is adult learning important in Latin America?

Globalisation and rapid technological change, together with demographic developments have considerably changed skill demands and supply in many OECD countries and partner countries and economies in the last decade. These trends are expected to continue in the coming years at an increasing pace. While in Latin America some of these structural megatrends are not yet fully realised – the pace of digitalisation, for instance, has been slower in the region than in the most advanced OECD economies - other structural factors such as demographic dynamics and informality are having an impact on skills imbalances. This chapter addresses these issues providing evidence on the main challenges facing Latin America and highlighting the importance of developing an adequately skilled workforce.

Summary of the main results

Technological progress is profoundly transforming the world of work, posing threats and opportunities that Latin American and the Caribbean (LAC) countries will face in the near future

- Recent OECD estimates suggest that on average across Chile, Ecuador, Mexico and Peru 24% of jobs will face a high risk of automation. This figure is around 9 percentage points higher than across OECD countries. An additional 35% of jobs in the region are likely to experience significant changes in the tasks that workers carry out daily, a figure that is approximately 5 percentage points higher than the OECD average.
- Employment in potentially automatable sectors is very high in Latin America. In Brazil, Chile, Colombia, Costa Rica, Mexico and Peru, the share of workers employed in highly automatable sectors such as manufacturing and agriculture ranges in between 30 and 40% of total employment.
- While many jobs could be "technically automatable", automation may not be yet economically attractive or viable for many firms in LAC economies as costly investments in advanced technology are usually out of reach to most entrepreneurs, especially for small and medium-sized enterprises (SMEs) in the region. This leaves room for policy makers in LAC countries to anticipate the potential change and react accordingly by developing today the skills that the workforce will need in the future.

Demographic dynamics are also crucial for skills development

- Population ageing is likely to put considerable pressure on education and training systems as it increases the need for individuals to maintain and update their skills over the life-course in the context of longer working lives. In Latin America, a large proportion of the region's population is still young (aged between 15 and 29), creating a demographic dividend. This window of opportunity, however, may be closing soon as the absolute number of young people is expected to fall after 2020.
- Brazil and Chile are projected to have a higher old-age dependency ratio than most OECD and G20 countries by 2075. This puts considerable pressure on education and training systems and increasing the need for individuals to maintain and update their skills over the life-course. The retirement of large cohorts can lead to significant shortages of qualified labour in some countries; a gap that can only be filled through the constant training of the existing workforce and the creation of effective adult learning systems.
- In Latin America, the weak participation of older workers in adult training along with the foreseen introduction of new technologies requiring the re-skilling and up-skilling of the workforce are going to put increasing pressure on labour markets and, potentially, magnify economy-wide skill and social divides.

Job quality and informality are major concerns in Latin America

- Workers in Latin America also tend to be more vulnerable to labour market risks than their counterparts in more advanced economies. High and persistent informal employment represents also a major policy concern, this latter ranging in between 9% in Uruguay and 65% in Guatemala.
- Workers in the informal sector have limited access to training opportunities, a situation that further exacerbates inequalities and penalise them when acquiring skills relative to workers in formal jobs.

- In all LAC countries, the probability of being employed in the informal sector decreases dramatically with the level of education of a worker. In Colombia, for instance, recent evidence points to skill upgrading as a major driver of the reduction in informality from 70% in 2007 to 62% in 2017.
- The low skills of many LAC employers and, in particular, the shortage of educated entrepreneurs in the informal sector, play a fundamental role in driving informality, much more important than the lack of demand in the economy. Much needs to be done to strengthen the skills of employers in the informal economy in Latin America to ensure that they play a key role in developing an effective adult learning response to the challenges of the future.
- In Guatemala and Brazil respectively only 8% and 13% of managers in the informal sector have a college degree. Boosting the number of well-educated entrepreneurs could contribute significantly to reduce the number of informal firms.

Despite substantial progress in recent years, the educational attainment and the skill levels of Latin America's population remain low by international standards

- Improving the coverage and the quality of LAC education systems is key but challenges lie ahead: only 64.2% of individuals aged 25-34 years old in the region has completed secondary education. This figure is about 20 percentage points lower than the OECD average (84%).
- Around 24% of 25-34 year-olds holds a tertiary degree (43% on average across OECD countries), suggesting that both enrolment rates of secondary and tertiary education need to be boosted to promote the further upskilling of the workforce.

The relatively poor quality of LAC's education and training systems also represents a key challenge in many LAC countries

- The OECD's Programme for International Student Assessment (PISA) measures 15-year-olds' proficiency in reading, mathematics and science to meet real-life challenges. Across many LAC countries, PISA scores are substantially below the OECD average and that of other emerging economies. The socio-economic background of students plays a prominent role in students' scores in LAC, much more than on average across OECD countries.
- In Peru, the socio-economic status of students explains more than 20% of the variability in PISA scores in science. Socio-economic status plays a great role also in Chile, Costa Rica and Colombia where its impact is well above that observed on average across OECD countries.
- Progress has been made in the last decade in many LAC countries to ensure that education and training systems are more inclusive and to boost their quality for students of all backgrounds. Some countries, however, are still struggling. In Chile and Colombia, for instance, the importance of socio-economic background in explaining students' performance has increased considerably in between 2006 and 2015.

Evidence highlights how LAC countries need to boost participation in high-quality training and, especially, in adult learning where LAC are lagging particularly behind

- The Survey of Adult Skills (PIAAC) shows that in many countries in the region (Chile, Ecuador, Mexico and Peru), on average, up to 60% of adults have low levels of skills – both in terms of literacy and numeracy proficiency. This calls for immediate action to boost the participation in up-skilling and learning activities for many adults in the region.

A large share of employment in LAC economies is found in low to medium-tech sectors, which is reflected in the demand for skills in the labour market

- In countries such as Argentina, Brazil, Chile, Mexico or Peru the shortages of highly skilled professionals is significantly lower than the OECD average, with less than 2 out of 10 jobs in shortage being "high-skilled" and the majority of jobs in demand being found, instead, in medium to low-skilled occupations.
- Evidence suggests that occupational shortages in LAC countries are mostly concentrated in low to medium-skill jobs in the agriculture and manufacturing sector and that. Certain shortages of skilled workers also emerge, but the demand is relatively weak.

Occupational and skill shortages are rather heterogeneous across countries and call for tailored policy intervention, boosting adult learning participation in the region

- In Chile, labourers in the mining and construction sector have experienced robust wage growth signalling a strong demand for low-medium workers in the country. At the same time, business and administration professionals have also seen a sharp increase in both their hours worked and wages, implying a sustained demand for these medium-skilled professionals.
- In Brazil, where the largest demand is in middle-skill professionals, health associate professional and personal care workers have been on the rise in recent years, while wages have been declining in traditionally high-skilled occupations such as science and engineering professionals, signalling a decrease in demand.
- Technical skills are in strong demand in both Mexico and Chile while Argentina's shortages are in social as well as in basic and complex problem solving skills. Surpluses of complex problem solving skills are instead found in relatively less developed economies such as Peru where demand for high-level skills is weak.

Factors affecting and reshaping skill demands in Latin America

Technology and demographics are shaping skill demands and mismatches in Latin America

The risk of automation in Latin America is potentially higher than across other OECD countries

Two major trends will affect the future of work globally and in Latin America: technological change and population ageing. Technological progress is already profoundly transforming the world of work and, as such, the skills demanded by employers around the world. While, on the one hand, new technologies have the potential to free up workers' time to do carry out productive and less routine-intensive tasks, on the other hand, they will likely change the nature of many jobs and the skills demanded to workers to perform them.

One particular aspect of technological change that has recently captured the attention of policy makers around the globe is that of automation. While certain degree of uncertainty in the estimation of the risk of automation remains, recent estimates (OECD, 2019[1]) report that 14% of jobs across OECD countries participating in the Survey of Adult Skills (PIAAC) are potentially highly automatable (i.e. probability of automation of over 70%). This is equivalent to over 66 million workers in the 32 countries covered by the study. Moreover, another 32% of jobs have a risk of between 50% and 70% pointing to the possibility of significant change in the way these jobs will be carried out as a result of automation.

Several dimensions are likely to affect the penetration of technology in a country and, as such, the risk of job automation. These factors include regulations on workers dismissal, unit labour costs or social preferences with regard to automation. Productive structure is likely to play an important role in the potential impact of technology and automation on job creation or destruction. Recent estimates confirms, in fact, that about 30% of the cross-country variance in the risk of automation is explained by cross-country differences in the structure of economic sectors (OECD, 2019[1]) and several analysts have found positive relationships between automation and job growth in the service sector but, in parallel, job destruction primarily in manufacturing.

While the literature on the impact of automation on jobs has largely focused on advanced economies, it is important to notice that emerging economies, such as LAC countries, start from very different initial conditions than more developed OECD countries. These include a different occupational mix, higher costs of information and communication technologies (ICT) capital, and greater skills shortages (Maloney and Molina, 2016[2]).

Based on their current stage of development, a large share of employment in emerging economies is found in sectors such as manufacturing and agriculture that could potentially face high risk of automation when new technologies are introduced in production activities.

In several LAC countries, for instance Brazil, Chile, Colombia, Costa Rica, Mexico and Peru, the share of workers employed in highly automatable sectors such as manufacturing and agriculture ranges in between 30% and 40% of total employment (Figure 2.1).

Figure 2.1. Agriculture and industry sectors make up a large share of employment in LAC

Employment in industry and agriculture (% of total employment), 2017

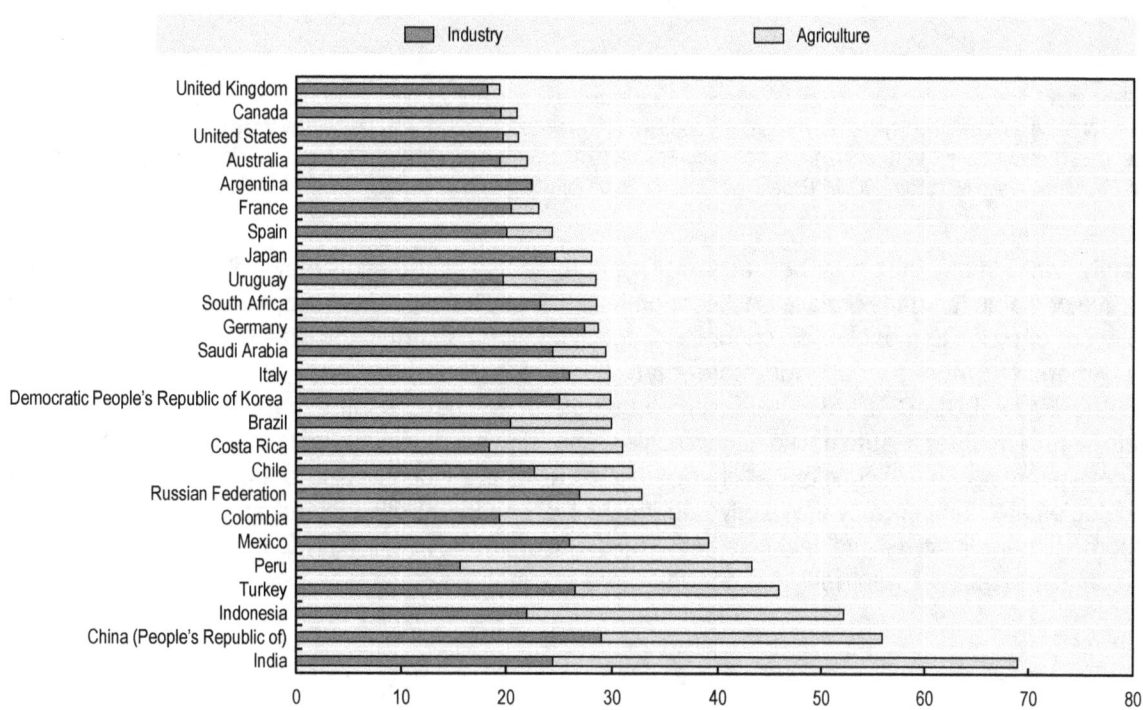

Source: The World Bank (2018[3]), World Development Indicators, http://datatopics.worldbank.org/world-development-indicators/.

Recent OECD estimates based on Nedelkoska and Quintini (2018[4]) suggests, in fact, that in Chile, Ecuador, Mexico and Peru,[1] an average of 23.6% of jobs face a high risk of automation. This is around

9 percentage points higher than across OECD countries, where more than 15% of jobs are, on average, facing a high risk of automation. Furthermore, in LAC countries for which information is available, an additional 35.1% of jobs are likely to experience significant changes in the tasks that workers carry out daily, a figure that is approximately 5 percentage points higher than the OECD average (Figure 2.2).

Similar results are found in other recent studies (The World Bank, 2016[5]; Weller, Gontero and Campbell, 2019[6]; McKinsey Global Institute, 2017[7]).[2]

Figure 2.2. A large share of jobs are at high risk of automation or significant change

Percentage of jobs at significant or high risk of automation

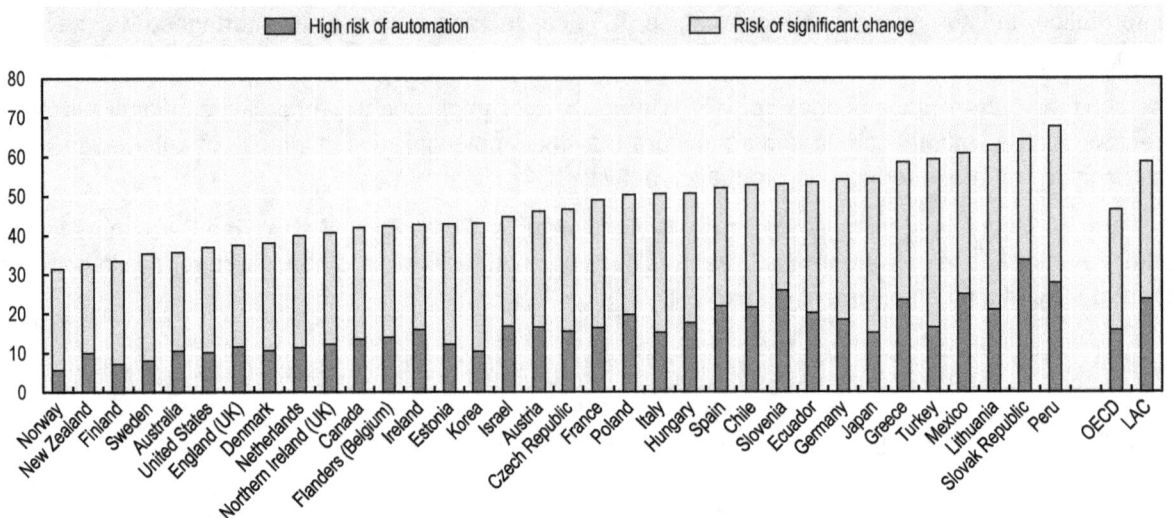

Note: Jobs are at high risk of automation if their likelihood to be automated is at least 70%. Jobs at risk of significant change are those with the likelihood of being automated estimated at between 50% and 70%. The values for "OECD" are weighted averages.
Source: OECD calculations based on estimates from Nedelkoska, L. and G. Quintini (2018[4]), "Automation, skills use and training", *OECD Social, Employment and Migration Working Papers*, No. 202, https://doi.org/10.1787/2e2f4eea-en.

Certainly, while many jobs may be "technically automatable", automation may not be yet economically attractive or viable for many firms in LAC economies as costly investments in sophisticated technology are usually out of reach to most entrepreneurs, especially in small and medium-sized enterprises (SMEs). In Latin America, SMEs account for more than 80% of employment and more than 90% of firms (OECD/CAF/UN ECLAC, 2016[8]) and such massive presence of SMEs has, until now, limited the penetration of high-end automating technologies and slowed down the potential risks for low skilled workers stemming from technological change. As of now, the incentives to adopt automation-intensive technologies are hampered by the relative abundance of cheap unskilled labour and by the lack of skilled workforce to benefit from digital technologies. The situation, however, is likely to change in the near future as automation becomes relatively cheaper and more efficient (Box 2.1).

> **Box 2.1. When will automation invest Latin America and other emerging economies?**
>
> It could take considerable time for the productivity gains from new technologies to be realised in emerging economies such as LAC countries. The past has seen unrealistic enthusiasm regarding timescales for the delivery of some industrial technologies. In some cases, as with nanotechnology, this reflects miscalculation of the technical challenges. And many technologies, such as big data and the Internet of Things, have developed in a wave-like pattern, with periods of rapid inventive activity coming after periods of slower activity and vice versa (OECD, 2015[9]). In terms of adoption, advanced ICTs remain below potential across OECD countries. By one estimate "the full shift to Industry 4.0 could take 20 years" (Lorenz et al., 2015[10]). The mere availability of a technology is not sufficient for its uptake and successful use and realising the benefits of a technology often requires that it be bundled with investments in complementary intangible assets, such as new skills and organisational forms, and that better adapted business models are invented that channel income to innovators.
>
> Successful absorption of new technologies in emerging and developing countries could help to achieve productivity, structural transformation and environmental goals. Indeed, some new production technologies are well suited to economic conditions in many developing countries. For example, certain state-of-the-art robots are relatively inexpensive and do not require highly skilled operators and low-cost drones could make some agricultural processes more efficient. With improved channels of knowledge diffusion, such as the Internet, opportunities for technological "leapfrogging" could emerge, particularly in large developing economies but the learning curve needed to use new technologies is clearly a challenge for companies in many developing economies.
>
> Source: OECD (2017[11]), *The Next Production Revolution: Implications for Governments and Business*, http://dx.doi.org/10.1787/9789264271036-en.

Demographic changes and population ageing are also affecting skills needs

The world's population is ageing. In Latin America, a large proportion of the region's population is, however, still young (aged between 15 and 29), creating a demographic dividend which has the potential for dramatic increases in productivity, savings, and economic growth. These windows of opportunity, however, may be closing soon as the absolute number of young people is expected to fall after 2020 and the relative share of young people over population aged 30 and more will continue the decline that has already started a few decades ago.

In Latin America, demographic conditions are therefore expected to shift towards a less favorable scenario entailing mounting pressure on public budgets and pension systems (OECD/CAF/UN ECLAC, 2016[8]).[3] In particular, the low dependency ratios[4] that LAC countries are experiencing nowadays are set to increase strongly in the next decades putting pressure on younger cohorts. To give an example, countries such as Brazil or Chile are projected to have a higher dependency rate than most OECD and G20 countries by 2075 (Table 2.1), posing questions about the sustainability of pension systems, productivity and economic growth.

Table 2.1. Old-age dependency ratios: Historical and projected values, 1950-2075

	1950	1975	2000	2015
OECD	**13.9**	**19.5**	**22.5**	**27.9**
Argentina	7.5	14.1	18.6	19.5
Brazil	6.5	8.0	9.3	13.0
Chile	8.6	11.3	13.1	17.0
Mexico	7.9	9.6	10.0	11.4
China (People's Republic of)	8.5	8.8	11.4	14.5
India	6.4	7.6	8.7	10.0
Indonesia	8.6	7.9	8.7	8.7
Russian Federation	8.7	15.5	20.4	20.7
Saudi Arabia	7.5	7.6	6.1	4.8
South Africa	8.5	8.1	7.8	9.0
EU28	14.7	21.2	24.3	29.9

Note: The demographic old-age dependency ratio is defined as the number of individuals aged 65 and over per 100 people of working age defined as those aged between 20 and 64.
Source: Adapted from United Nations, Department of Economic and Social Affairs, Population Division (2019[12]), *World Population Prospects 2019: Highlights (ST/ESA/SER.A/423)*, https://population.un.org/wpp/Publications/Files/WPP2019_Highlights.pdf.

From a skills development point of view, an ageing population is an often-overlooked driver of changing skill demand and supply (OECD, 2019[13]). An ageing population can have substantial impacts on a country's skills supply and training needs in a number of important ways. To start with, population ageing is likely to put considerable pressure on education and training systems as it increases the need for individuals to maintain and update their skills over the life-course in the context of longer working lives. In Latin America, the weak participation of older workers in adult training, coupled with large margins for the introduction of new technologies requiring re-skilling and up-skilling is deemed to put increasing pressure on labour markets and magnify economy-wide skill gaps. In addition, in the context of an increase old-dependency ratio, the retirement of large cohorts can lead to significant shortages of qualified labour in some countries; a gap that can be filled through training of the existing workforce amongst other measures (OECD, 2019[13]). Finally, population ageing is likely to contribute to additional changes in the structure of the economy, leading for instance to increase in the consumption of specific goods and services, an example being an increased demand for health and elderly care services which will require the development of specific skills to fill gaps in the labour market.

Labour market conditions: Job quality and informality are barriers to developing effective labour markets and so an obstacle to skill development

Job quality in Latin America tends to be low

Job quality, in the form of earnings, labour market security and the quality of the working environment can raise well-being, foster productivity while reducing labour market inequalities (Cazes, Hijzen and Saint-Martin, 2015[14]). Nonetheless, job quality is a major concern in Latin America (Figure 2.3). Lower earnings quality compared to the OECD average reflect both substantially lower average earnings and higher levels of earnings inequality. Workers in Latin America also tend to be more vulnerable to labour market risks than their counterparts in more advanced economies. In most emerging economies, this primarily reflects the risk of falling into extreme low pay. The quality of the working environment is also generally lower in Latin America compared with OECD countries. One indication of this is the higher incidence of working very long hours (OECD, 2015[15]).

Figure 2.3. Job quality in LAC countries is low compared to other OECD countries

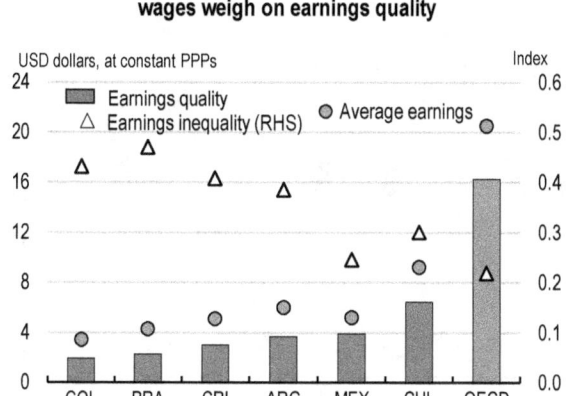
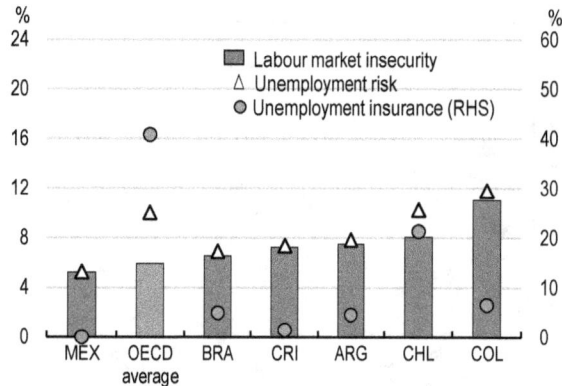

Note: Data are for 2010, except for Brazil (2009), Chile (2011 for labour market insecurity and 2013 for earnings quality) and Mexico (2013). The OECD average is a simple cross-country average in 2013. OECD calculations based on national household and labour force surveys (EPH: Argentina, PNAD: Brazil, CASEN: Chile, GEIH: Colombia, ENHAO: Costa Rica, ENIGH: Mexico). Earnings quality refers to the extent to which the earnings received by workers in their jobs contribute to their well-being by taking account both the average level as well as the distribution, and can be interpreted as the hourly earnings in USD adjusted for inequality. Labour market insecurity measures the risk of unemployment (the risk of becoming unemployed and the expected duration of unemployment) and the degree of public unemployment insurance (coverage of benefits and their generosity), and can interpreted as the expected monetary loss associated with becoming and staying unemployed as a share of previous earnings. For Argentina, Brazil, Colombia and Costa Rica unemployment insurance is measured as the ratio of the average net income of the unemployed relative to the median net earnings among the employed, and the risk of becoming unemployed is approximated by the unemployment rate, due to limited data availability.
Source: OECD (2014[16]), *OECD Employment Outlook 2014*, https://doi.org/10.1787/empl_outlook-2014-en; OECD (2016[17]), "Job quality" *OECD.Stat* (database), http://stats.oecd.org.

Training and adult learning can play a fundamental role in lifting workers out of informality

High and persistent informal employment represents a major policy concern and greatly complicates the challenge of promoting strong productivity growth and more inclusive labour markets in Latin America. Informality, the share of wage earners and self-employed without contributions to the pension system, slightly decreased in the region over the last decade but it remains pervasive across many LAC countries ranging from about 9% in Uruguay to around 65% in Guatemala (Figure 2.4).

Informality is widespread across very different groups of workers, including own-account workers, family workers and self-employed, but also unregistered wage employees in formal or informal firms (OECD, 2009[18]). Moreover, disadvantaged individuals such as low-skilled youth, women or older workers are much more likely to work informally with important repercussions on their earnings and options for skill development.

Evidence shows that workers in informal jobs can earn less than workers in formal jobs, regardless of their socio-economic background and or individual characteristics such as qualification level (ILO, 2016[19]).

From a skill development point of view, informality represents an important challenge. Workers in the informal sector have, in fact, reduced access to training opportunities, a situation that further exacerbates inequalities and penalise them relative to workers in formal jobs when acquiring skills (Carpio et al., 2011[20]).

Figure 2.4. Informality is still pervasive in the LAC region

Informally employed persons as a % of the working-age employment (latest year available)

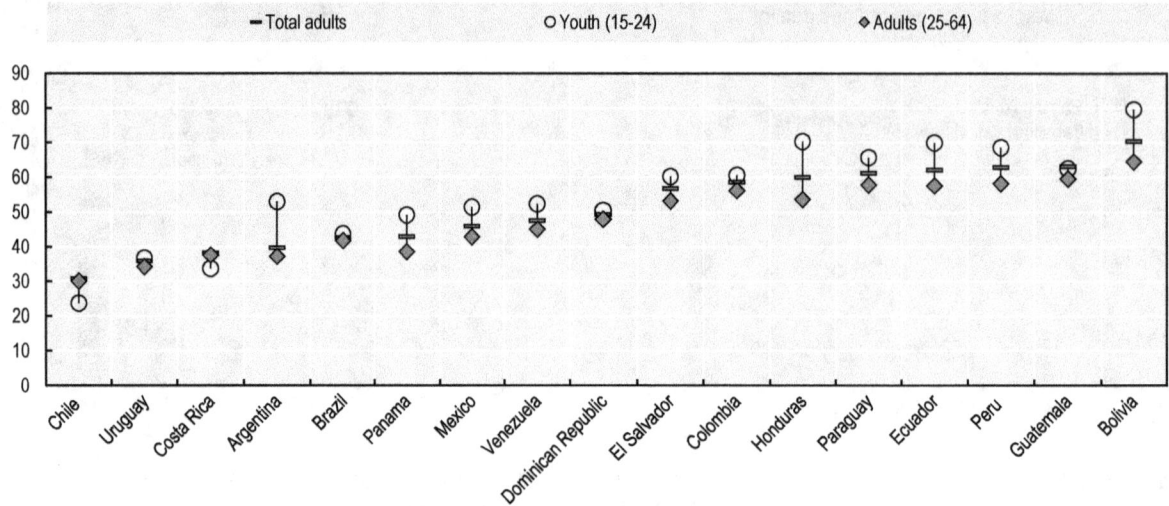

Source: Adapted from CEDLAS and The World Bank (2019[21]), Socio-Economic Database for Latin America and the Caribbean, http://www.cedlas.econo.unlp.edu.ar/wp/en/estadisticas/sedlac/.

Skills development and informality are linked in a two-way relationship where informal firms tend to be less productive as they generally hire less skilled workers and skilled workers have fewer incentives to be employed in informal firms. Lower participation in training among informal workers is due, in large part to the reduced incentives and capacity that their employers have to provide training (OECD et al., 2019[22]).

If informality hinders skills development, boosting the skills and training opportunities for both employees and employers can play a fundamental role in reducing informality. Recent evidence (IMF, 2018[23]) highlights, in fact, that in all countries in the LAC region, the probability of being employed in the informal sector decreases dramatically with the level of education of a worker.

For instance, in Colombia, recent evidence points to skill upgrading explaining two-thirds of the reduction in informality from 70% in 2007 to 62% in 2017 (IMF, 2018[23]).[5] In particular, a worker with a postgraduate degree is nine times as likely to be formal than a worker without any education, and twice as likely as a worker with a high school degree, but no tertiary education.

Equally important are the skills of employers as evidence shows that they play a fundamental role in driving informality. La Porta and Shleifer (2014[24]) argue, for instance, that the lack of human capital, and in particular, the shortage of educated entrepreneurs in the informal sector might be the most important driver of informality, much more important than lack of demand in the economy. World Bank data on a set of developing countries report that, on average, only 7% of the managers of informal firms have a college degree against 76% of employers in formal firms. In Guatemala and Brazil only 8% and 13%, respectively, of managers in the informal sector have a college degree but boosting this number could contribute significantly to reduce the number of informal firms.

Educational attainment and outcomes remain low in the LAC region for both young and adult individuals

Developing strong basic skills in initial education is key to foster participation in further education and training. LAC countries have made substantial progress in improving the coverage and the quality of their education systems, particularly at the primary level (OECD/CAF/UN ECLAC, 2016[8]). Nonetheless, important challenges remain ahead. The low quantity of students enrolled in education and the poor quality of courses are two interrelated challenges in Latin America.

The educational attainment and the skills level of Latin America's population remain low by international standards. Only 64.2% of individuals aged 25-34 years old have completed secondary education, a figure that is about 20 percentage points lower than the OECD average (84%). In addition, only 23.9% of 25-34 year-olds hold a tertiary degree (43% on average across OECD countries) (Figure 2.5), suggesting that both enrolment rates of secondary and tertiary education need to be boosted to promote the further upskilling of the workforce.

Figure 2.5. Latin America needs to continue to raise educational attainment

Share of population (23-34 year-olds) having completed, % 2017 or latest available year

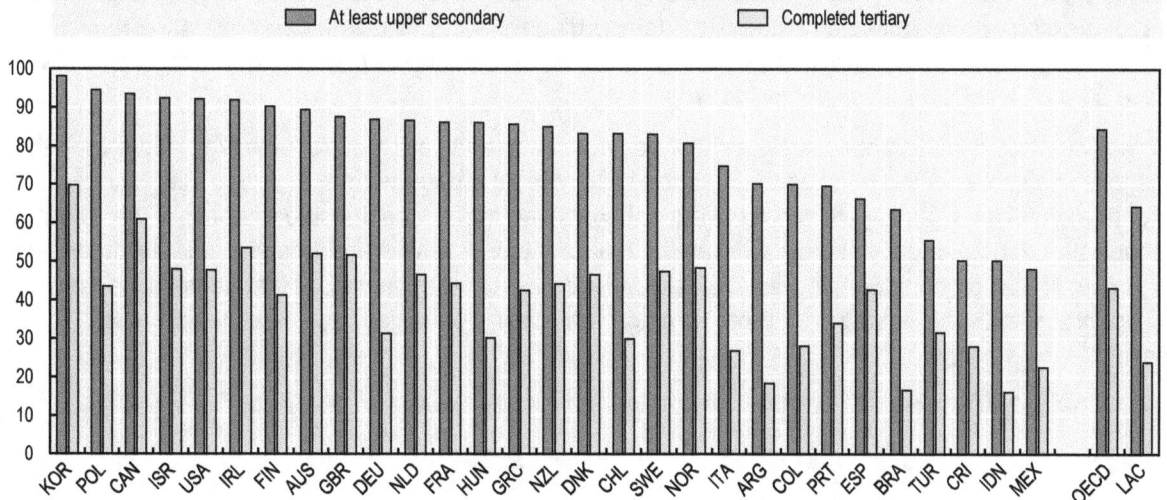

Source: OECD (2019[25]), "Education at a Glance", OECD.Stat (database), http://stats.oecd.org.

Solely increasing the quantity of individuals enrolled in education is, however, going to be insufficient to address the pressing challenges facing Latin America's skill system. LAC countries need to step up their effort to strengthen the quality of education courses as well as that of their adult learning systems.

The OECD's Programme for International Student Assessment (PISA) measures 15-year-olds' ability to use their reading, mathematics and science knowledge and skills to meet real-life challenges. PISA scores provide a good approximation of how education and training systems are effective in developing students' skills. Across many LAC countries, PISA scores in science, but also in mathematics and reading, are substantially below the OECD average, as well as below the level of other emerging economies.

The share of low performers is also considerably higher than the OECD average: more than half of young Latin Americans has not acquired basic-level proficiency (OECD/CAF/UN ECLAC, 2016[8]). Participation in early childhood education plays an important role in students' performance later on (Box 2.2).

Students' socio-economic backgrounds also influence their opportunities to benefit from education and develop their skills. These associations partly reflect the advantages in resources that relatively high socio-economic status confers. For example, at the system level, high socio-economic status is often related to greater wealth and higher spending on education. At the school level, socio-economic status tends to be positively correlated with a range of community characteristics that can boost student performance, such as a safe environment or the availability of public libraries and museums. At the individual level, socio-economic status can be related to parents' attitudes towards education, in general, and to their involvement in their child's education, in particular. In Peru, socio-economic status explains more than 20% of the variability in PISA scores in science, but socio-economic status plays a great role also in Chile, Costa Rica and Colombia where its impact is well above the average across OECD countries (Figure 2.6). In contrast to other LAC countries, in Chile and Colombia, the importance of socio-economic background in explaining students' performance has also increased considerably in between 2006 and 2015.

> **Box 2.2. Participation in early childhood education plays an important role in students' performance later on**
>
> Participation in early childhood education and care (ECEC) varies significantly across countries, despite the evidence that engagement in such activities has a strong impact on students' cognitive and non-cognitive skills development. In particular, recent studies show that high-quality ECEC can result in better outcomes in subsequent stages of life and disadvantaged children can benefit the most from attending high-quality early childhood education. Later interventions are less efficient because they take place after children's "development window".
>
> Increasing rates of participation in early childhood education and care require, however, addressing the financial costs that act too often as the main barrier preventing parents from enrolling their children. To encourage universal participation in initial education, governments can consider measures that enforce school attendance, target students who are at risk of lagging behind and design targeted measures regarding school dropout. Such measures need to be combined with measures that address inequalities of opportunities. The engagement of parents, the local authorities but also teachers as main stakeholders is crucial.
>
> Source: OECD (2019[13]), *OECD Skills Strategy 2019: Skills to Shape a Better Future*, https://doi.org/10.1787/9789264313835-en.

Figure 2.6. School results and equity remain a challenge

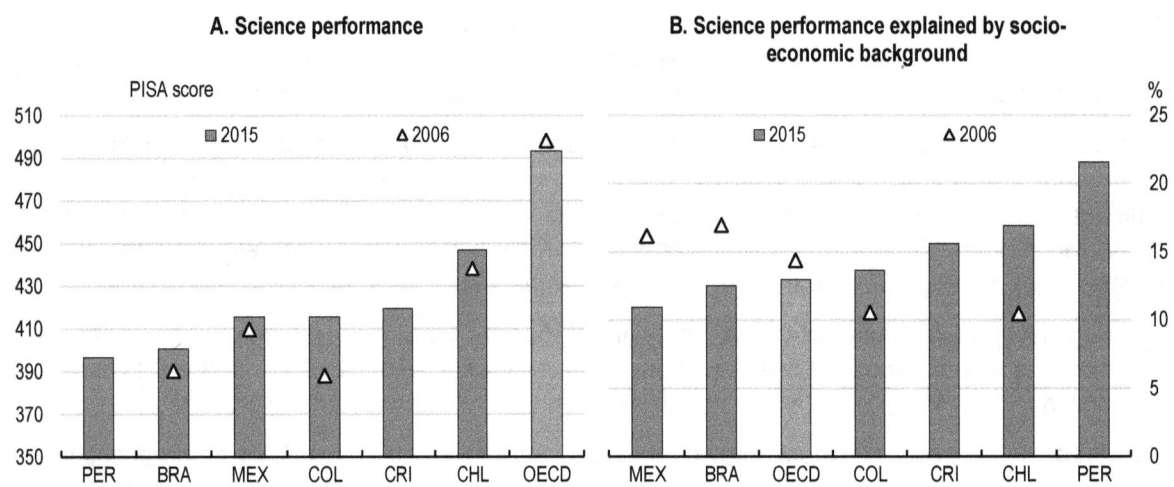

Note: Panel B displays the percentage of variation in science performance explained by the PISA index of economic, social and cultural.
Source: OECD (2006[26]), *PISA 2006 Database*, https://www.oecd.org/pisa/pisaproducts/database-pisa2006.htm; OECD (2015[27]), *PISA 2015 Database*, http://www.oecd.org/pisa/data/2015database/.

Negative education outcomes early in life as students translate into poor skill developments as adults. Analysis of data from the Survey of Adult Skills (PIAAC) shows that in the LAC region (Chile, Ecuador, Mexico and Peru), more than 60% of adults have low levels of skills – both in terms of literacy and numeracy. This figure is three times larger than the OECD average (Figure 2.7).

Evidence highlights how LAC countries need to boost participation in high quality training at all levels and especially in adult learning where LAC are lagging particularly behind.

Providing learning opportunities to adults in Latin America can therefore play a crucial role in developing the necessary skills needed to face the challenges of the future of work and in revamping stagnant productivity growth in Latin America while promoting more inclusive labour markets and societies.

Figure 2.7. The proportion of low performers in literacy and numeracy

Adults

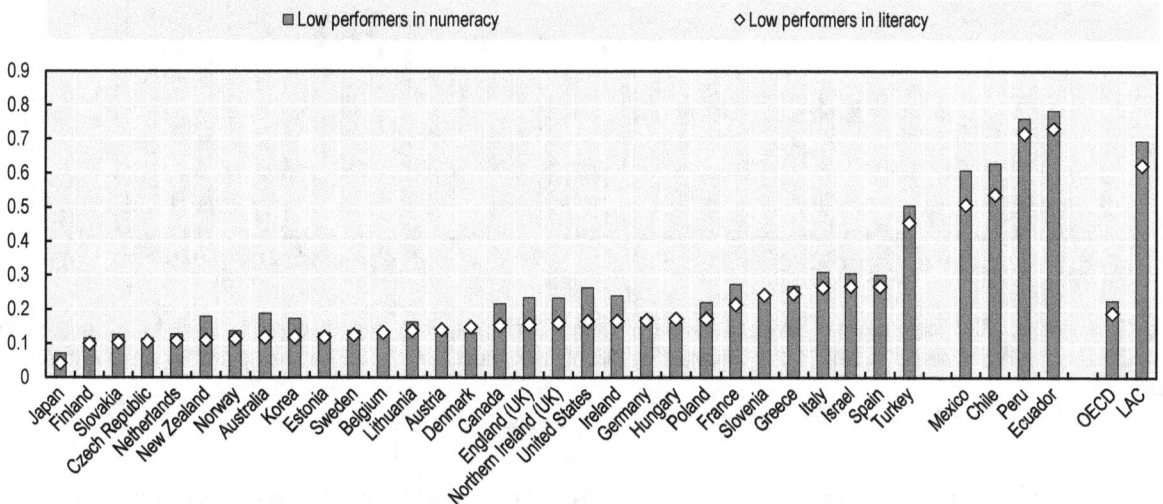

Note: Low-performers are defined as those who score at or below level 1 in in either literacy or numeracy.
According to the Survey of Adult Skills (PIAAC). Hungary, Mexico, the United States, Ecuador and Peru: Year of reference 2017. Chile, Greece, Israel, New Zealand, Slovenia and Turkey: Year of reference 2015. All other countries: Year of reference 2012. Data for Belgium refer only to Flanders and data for the United Kingdom refer to England and Northern Ireland jointly.
Source: OECD calculations based on OECD (2017[28]), Survey of Adults Skills (PIAAC) (2012, 2015, 2017) (database), http://www.oecd.org/skills/piaac/.

The economic development of LAC countries shapes their skill demands and imbalances

The productive and sectoral distribution of employment of LAC countries combined with recent pressing demographic developments and the relatively poor skill proficiency of the adult population in the region are reflected in the emerging skills imbalances (shortages, surpluses and mismatches) across labour markets.

Measures of skill imbalances are often issued from employer surveys, which include questions on hiring intentions and recruitment difficulties. According to the *Talent Shortage Survey* by Manpower group, many LAC countries experience gaps between the available pool of skills and those skills that economies and societies require (Figure 2.8 Panel A).[6] According to the same survey, employers cited low numbers of applicants, lack of technical competencies, lack of experience, and lack of soft skills as reasons contributing to the difficulty of filling open positions (ManpowerGroup, 2015[29]).

Moreover, based on the *World Bank Enterprise Survey 2009-2017*, approximately a third of firms (32%) in Latin America identified an inadequately educated workforce as a constraint to their activity.

Figure 2.8. Finding the right skills can be difficult in Latin America (Employer reported labour market imbalances)

Share of firms identifying hiring difficulty, 2017

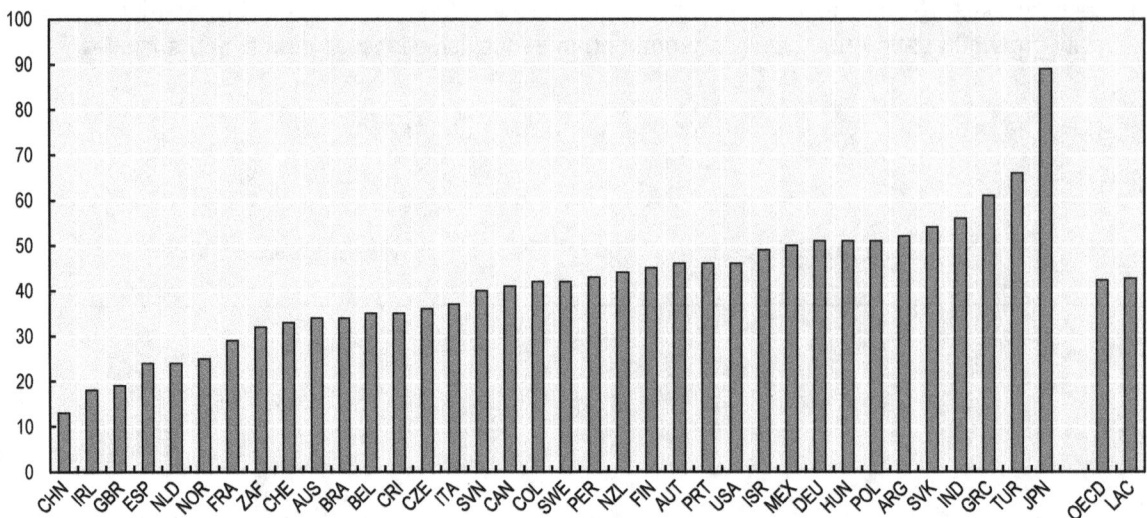

Note: Data refer to 2017 for Argentina, Bolivia, Colombia, Ecuador, Guatemala, Peru and Uruguay; to 2016 for El Salvador, the Dominican Republic and Honduras; to 2010 for the Bolivarian Republic of Venezuela, Chile, Costa Rica, Mexico and Panama and to 2009 for Brazil.
Source: ManpowerGroup (2017[30]), Talent Shortage Survey, https://go.manpowergroup.com/talent-shortage.

While these results suggest that shortages in Latin America are significant, they need to be interpreted with caution, as they rely on self-reported subjective perceptions of a very selected sample of employers (i.e. formal firms in manufacturing).

A different approach to the measurement of skills imbalances has been recently proposed in the OECD Skills for Jobs database[7] which provides detailed information about the skill needs of the labour markets (see Box 2.3 for more details). The indicator is built by tracking a multidimensional set of quantitative and objective (rather than subjective) indicators for each occupational group of the labour market. Indicators include wage growth, employment growth and unemployment and provide an assessment of the demand by the labour market for specific occupations and their associated skills.

Evidence shows that, on average across OECD countries, more than 5 out of 10 jobs that are hard to fill (i.e. in shortage) are found in high-skilled occupations (Figure 2.9). These jobs range from managerial positions to highly skilled professionals in the health care, teaching or ICT sectors. A relatively large share of OECD occupational shortage (approximately 39% of total jobs that are hard-to-fill across OECD countries) is also found in medium-skilled occupations, such as personal service workers or electrical and electronic trades workers. Less than 1 out 10 jobs in shortage across OECD countries are found in low skilled occupations.

The picture is rather different for LAC countries. In countries such as Argentina, Brazil, Chile, Mexico and Peru the shortages of highly skilled professionals is significantly lower than the OECD average, with less than 2 out of 10 jobs in shortage being "high-skilled" and the majority of jobs in demand being found, instead, in medium to low-skilled occupations.

Results seem to suggest that the demand for employment in LAC countries is still mostly concentrated in low to medium-skill jobs in the agriculture and manufacturing sector and that, despite the overall skill supply of the region being relatively low, this is sufficient to meet an equally rather weak demand for high-skills.

> **Box 2.3. OECD Skills for Jobs database**
>
> The OECD Skills for Jobs database provides timely information about skills shortages – i.e. when skills sought by employers are not available in the pool of potential recruits – and skills surpluses – i.e. when the supply of certain skills is higher than the demand. The database has key innovative features compared to existing measures of skills shortages/surpluses. By looking at skills – i.e. the set of competences mobilised to perform the tasks related to a job – the new indicators go beyond the traditional measures of imbalances. Furthermore, unlike the generally subjective information available from employer surveys, the OECD Skills for Jobs database draws from quantitative data derived from household surveys. Finally, the indicator is constructed using a multidimensional set of quantitative signals on skills pressure (i.e. five sub-indices, including wage growth, employment growth and unemployment), which provides a holistic interpretation of skill imbalances in the labour markets. The skill needs indicator is constructed in two consecutive steps:
>
> - In the first step, sub-indices for hourly wage growth, employment growth, unemployment rate, hours worked and under-qualification are used to provide a quantitative indication of the extent of the labour market pressure on each one of the occupations analysed. The result of this analysis returns a ranking of occupations ordered from the one most in shortage to most in surplus.
> - In the second step, occupations that are in shortage/surplus are mapped into the underlying skills requirements associated to those occupations, using the occupation-skills taxonomy developed by O*NET.
>
> Information is provided at the 2-digit ISCO occupation level and is disaggregated into three domains of competence – knowledge, skills, and abilities:
>
> - Knowledge refers to the body of information that makes adequate performance on the job possible (e.g. knowledge of plumbing for a plumber; knowledge of mathematics for an economist).
> - Skills refer to the proficient manual, verbal or mental manipulation of data or things (e.g. complex problem solving; social skills).
> - Ability refer to the competence to perform an observable activity (e.g. ability to plan and organise work; attentiveness; endurance).
>
> The database covers most OECD countries and some emerging economies. LAC countries included in the database are: Argentina, Brazil, Chile, Mexico and Peru. Indicators are available at the regional and occupational level.
>
> Source: OECD (2017[31]), *Getting Skills Right: Skills for Jobs Indicators*, https://doi.org/10.1787/9789264277878-en.

Figure 2.9. Share of employment in high demand, by skills level

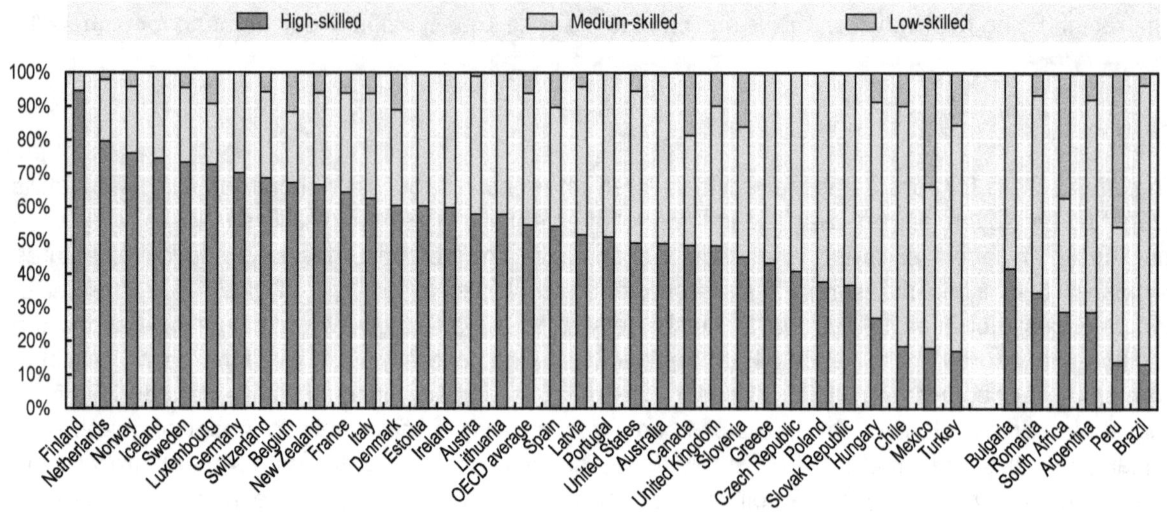

Source: OECD (2018[32]), OECD Skills for Jobs database, https://www.oecdskillsforjobsdatabase.org.

Results at the occupational level confirm that, in Latin America, shortages can be found in a variety of low-medium skill occupations such as assemblers or labourers in mining, construction, manufacturing and transport, customer service clerks but also in medium to high-level occupations such as ICT technicians and business and administration professionals.

Surpluses (i.e. occupations that have recently experienced a decline in wage growth or in hours worked for instance) can be observed in certain managerial occupations. These can be found in production and specialised services managers or chief executives, senior officials and legislator as well as in some occupational categories that may be more exposed to the effects of automation such as general and keyboard clerks or metal, machinery and related trades workers as well as sales workers.

The picture is, however, rather heterogeneous when one looks at the specifics of each country. For instance, in Chile, labourers in mining and construction,[8] have experienced robust wage growth signalling a strong demand for low-medium professionals in the country in those occupations. At the same time, also business and administration professionals have also seen a sharp increase in both hours worked and wages, implying a sustained demand for this medium-skilled professionals. In Brazil, where the largest demand is in middle-skill professionals, health associate professional and personal care workers have been on the rise in recent years, while wages have been declining in traditionally high-skilled occupations such as science and engineering professionals.[9]

The emergence of skills shortages and surpluses signals that labour markets are struggling to align skills supply to demand. The disconnect between the educational offer and labour market needs can lead to persistent skills and qualification mismatch (Figure 2.10) which, in turn, are likely to contribute to high wage inequality and low productivity in the region (OECD/CAF/UN ECLAC, 2016[8]).

Indicators of qualification mismatch are useful measures of the alignment of a worker's qualification level to that required in her/his job. So-called over-qualified workers own higher qualifications than usually required in their jobs while under-qualified workers have lower qualifications than those usually held by workers in similar jobs. Evidence from the OECD Skills for Jobs database reveals that, 44% of workers in Latin America are mismatched by qualification, in contrast to 35% across OECD countries.

Table 2.2. Occupational shortage and surplus in Latin America

Top 10 shortage occupations	Top 10 surplus occupations
Market-oriented skilled forestry, fishery and hunting workers	Production and specialised services managers
Personal care workers	Legal, social and cultural professionals
Customer services clerks	Metal, machinery and related trades workers
Assemblers	Chief executives, senior officials and legislators
Subsistence farmers, fishers, hunters and gatherers	Market-oriented skilled agricultural workers
Refuse workers and other elementary workers	Administrative and commercial managers
Information and communications technicians	Handicraft and printing workers
Labourers in mining, construction, manufacturing and transport	General and keyboard clerks
Protective services workers	Legal, social, cultural and related associate professionals
Business and administration associate professionals	Street and related sales and services workers

Note: Values are obtained by taking the average of the occupational indicators for Argentina, Brazil, Chile, Mexico and Peru, when available. Latest year available for each country.
Source: OECD (2018[32]), OECD Skills for Jobs database, https://www.oecdskillsforjobsdatabase.org.

Figure 2.10. Qualification mismatch is high in Latin America

Percentage of mismatched workers

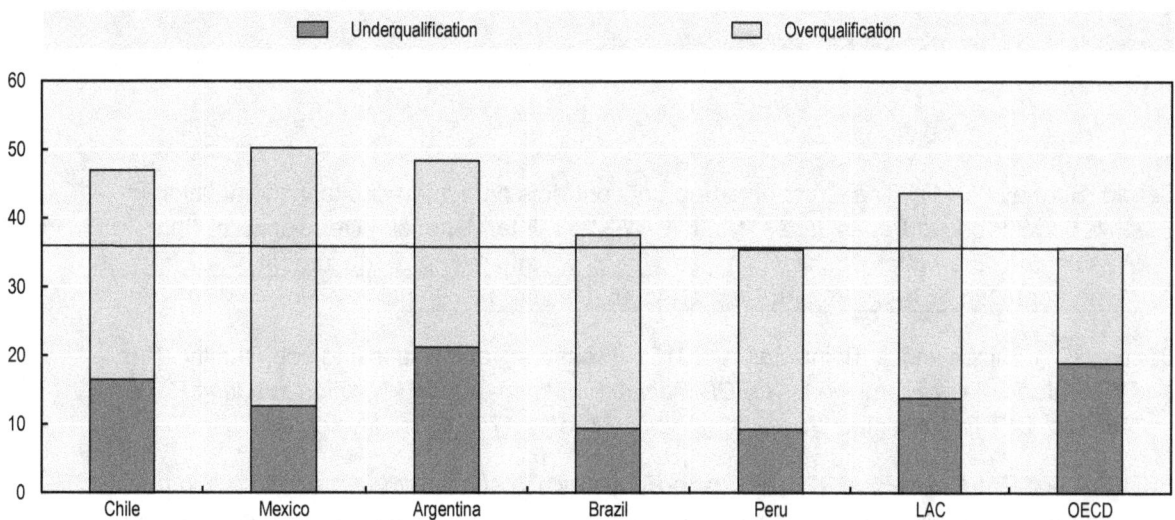

Note: Mismatch is calculated as the share of individuals with a higher (over-qualification) or lower (under-qualification) level of qualification than the modal level in his/her occupation.
Source: OECD (2018[32]), OECD Skills for Jobs database, https://www.oecdskillsforjobsdatabase.org.

Moreover, results show that LAC countries present a higher share of overqualified workers than across OECD countries (30% in Latin America vs. 17% across OECD countries) highlighting the relatively weak demand for high-level skills in economies that are still in their development phase and where there is ample room to boost the adoption of new technologies into the productive structure.

Further evidence from the OECD Skills for Jobs database show that skill demands are quite heterogeneous across the countries examined, reflecting differences in their productive structure, export pattern and internal demand. For instance, technical skills are in strong demand in both Chile and Mexico while Argentina's shortages are in social as well as in basic and complex problem solving skills. Surpluses of complex problem solving skills (signalling a weak demand) are instead found in relatively less developed economies such as Peru.

Figure 2.11. Skills shortage indicators for selected LAC and OECD countries

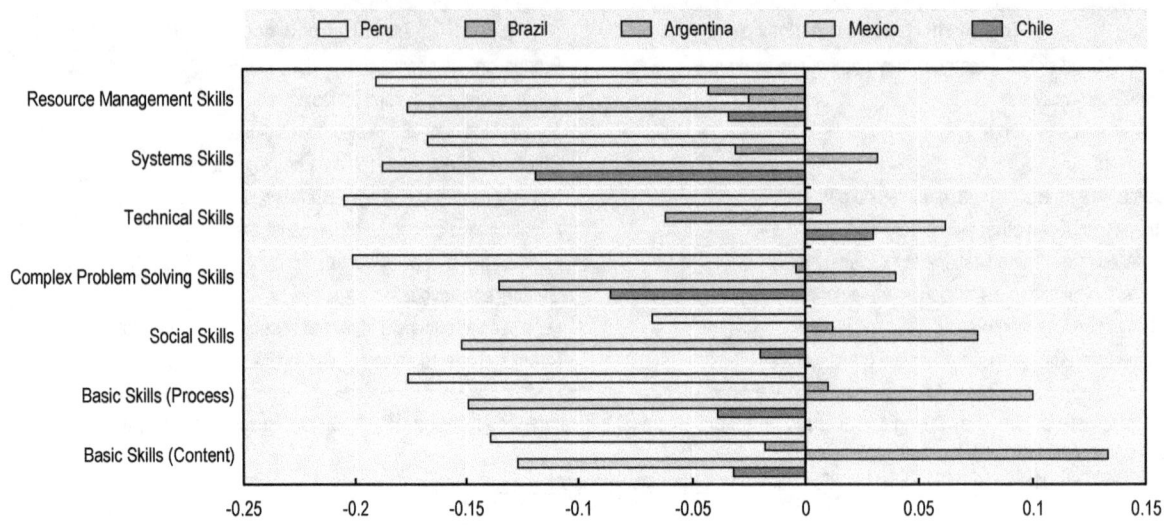

Note: Negative (positive) values indicate that a specific skill is in surplus (shortage). Values for Latin America are obtained by taking the average of the occupational indicators for Argentina, Brazil, Chile, Mexico and Peru. Values for the OECD are obtained by taking the average for all OECD countries included in the 2018 OECD Skills for Jobs database. Latest year available for each country.
Source: OECD (2018[32]), OECD Skills for Jobs database, https://www.oecdskillsforjobsdatabase.org.

References

Carpio, S. et al. (2011), "The effect of temporary contracts on human capital accumulation in Chile", *IDB Working Paper Series*, No. IDB-WP-253, Inter-American Development Bank, Washington, D.C., https://publications.iadb.org/publications/english/document/The-Effect-of-Temporary-Contracts-on-Human-Capital-Accumulation-in-Chile.pdf. [20]

Cazes, S., A. Hijzen and A. Saint-Martin (2015), "Measuring and Assessing Job Quality: The OECD Job Quality Framework", *OECD Social, Employment and Migration Working Papers*, No. 174, OECD Publishing, Paris, https://dx.doi.org/10.1787/5jrp02kjw1mr-en. [14]

CEDLAS and The World Bank (2019), *Socio-Economic Database for Latin America and the Caribbean*, http://www.cedlas.econo.unlp.edu.ar/wp/en/estadisticas/sedlac/ (accessed on 11 December 2019). [21]

Frey, C. and M. Osborne (2017), "The future of employment: How susceptible are jobs to computerisation?", *Technological Forecasting and Social Change*, Vol. 114, pp. 254-280, http://dx.doi.org/10.1016/j.techfore.2016.08.019. [33]

ILO (2016), *Non-standard Employment Around the World: Understanding Challenges, Shaping Prospects*, International Labour Office, Geneve, https://www.ilo.org/wcmsp5/groups/public/---dgreports/---dcomm/---publ/documents/publication/wcms_534326.pdf. [19]

IMF (2018), "Colombia : Selected Issues", *IMF Staff Country Reports*, No. 18/129, https://www.imf.org/en/Publications/CR/Issues/2018/05/29/Colombia-Selected-Issues-45899. [23]

La Porta, R. and A. Shleifer (2014), "Informality and development", *Journal of Economic Perspectives*, Vol. 28/3, pp. 109-26, https://www.aeaweb.org/articles?id=10.1257/jep.28.3.109. [24]

Lorenz, M. et al. (2015), *Man and machine in Industry 4.0: How will technology transform the industrial workforce through 2025?*, The Boston Consulting Group, https://www.bcg.com/publications/2015/technology-business-transformation-engineered-products-infrastructure-man-machine-industry-4.aspx. [10]

Maloney, W. and C. Molina (2016), "Are automation and trade polarizing developing country labor markets, too?", *Policy Research Working Paper*, No. WPS 7922, World Bank Group, Washington, D.C., http://documents.worldbank.org/curated/en/869281482170996446/Are-automation-and-trade-polarizing-developing-country-labor-markets-too. [2]

ManpowerGroup (2017), *Talent Shortage Survey*, ManpowerGroup, https://go.manpowergroup.com/talent-shortage. [30]

ManpowerGroup (2015), *Talent Shortage Survey*, https://go.manpowergroup.com/talent-shortage. [29]

McKinsey Global Institute (2017), *A Future that Works: Automation, Employment and Productivity*, McKinsey & Company, https://www.mckinsey.com/~/media/mckinsey/featured%20insights/Digital%20Disruption/Harnessing%20automation%20for%20a%20future%20that%20works/MGI-A-future-that-works-Full-report.ashx. [7]

Nedelkoska, L. and G. Quintini (2018), "Automation, skills use and training", *OECD Social, Employment and Migration Working Papers*, No. 202, OECD Publishing, Paris, https://doi.org/10.1787/2e2f4eea-en. [4]

OECD (2019), "Education at a Glance", *OECD.Stat (database)*, http://stats.oecd.org (accessed on 11 December 2019). [25]

OECD (2019), *OECD Employment Outlook 2019: The Future of Work*, OECD Publishing, Paris, https://dx.doi.org/10.1787/9ee00155-en. [1]

OECD (2019), *OECD Skills Strategy 2019: Skills to Shape a Better Future*, OECD Publishing, Paris, https://dx.doi.org/10.1787/9789264313835-en. [13]

OECD (2018), *OECD Skills for Jobs Database*, https://www.oecdskillsforjobsdatabase.org. [32]

OECD (2017), *Getting Skills Right: Skills for Jobs Indicators*, Getting Skills Right, OECD Publishing, Paris, https://dx.doi.org/10.1787/9789264277878-en. [31]

OECD (2017), *Survey of Adults Skills (PIAAC) (2012, 2015, 2017)*, (database), http://www.oecd.org/skills/piaac/. [28]

OECD (2017), *The Next Production Revolution: Implications for Governments and Business*, OECD Publishing, Paris, https://dx.doi.org/10.1787/9789264271036-en. [11]

OECD (2016), "Job quality", *OECD.Stat (database)*, http://stats.oecd.org (accessed on 11 December 2019). [17]

OECD (2015), *Data-Driven Innovation: Big Data for Growth and Well-Being*, OECD Publishing, Paris, https://dx.doi.org/10.1787/9789264229358-en. [9]

OECD (2015), "Enhancing job quality in emerging economies", in *OECD Employment Outlook 2015*, OECD Publishing, Paris, https://dx.doi.org/10.1787/empl_outlook-2015-9-en. [15]

OECD (2015), *PISA 2015 Database*, http://www.oecd.org/pisa/data/2015database/. [27]

OECD (2014), *OECD Employment Outlook 2014*, OECD Publishing, Paris, https://dx.doi.org/10.1787/empl_outlook-2014-en. [16]

OECD (2009), *OECD Employment Outlook 2009: Tackling the Jobs Crisis*, OECD Publishing, Paris, https://dx.doi.org/10.1787/empl_outlook-2009-en. [18]

OECD (2006), *OECD PISA 2006 Database*, https://www.oecd.org/pisa/pisaproducts/database-pisa2006.htm. [26]

OECD/CAF/UN ECLAC (2016), *Latin American Economic Outlook 2017: Youth, Skills and Entrepreneurship*, OECD Publishing, Paris, https://dx.doi.org/10.1787/leo-2017-en. [8]

OECD et al. (2019), *Latin American Economic Outlook 2019: Development in Transition*, OECD Publishing, Paris, https://dx.doi.org/10.1787/g2g9ff18-en. [22]

The World Bank (2018), *World Development Indicators*, http://datatopics.worldbank.org/world-development-indicators/. [3]

The World Bank (2016), *World Development Report 2016: Digital Dividends*, International Bank for Reconstruction and Development / The World Bank, Washington, DC, http://dx.doi.org/10.1596/978-1-4648-0728-2. [5]

United Nations, Department of Economic and Social Affairs, Population Division (2019), *World Population Prospects 2019: Highlights (ST/ESA/SER.A/423)*, United Nations, New York, https://population.un.org/wpp/Publications/Files/WPP2019_Highlights.pdf. [12]

Weller, J., S. Gontero and S. Campbell (2019), "Cambio tecnológico y empleo: una perspectiva latinoamericana. Riesgos de la sustitución tecnológica del trabajo humano y desafíos de la generación de nuevos puestos de trabajo", *Macroeconomía del Desarollo*, No. 201, CEPAL, https://www.cepal.org/es/publicaciones/44637-cambio-tecnologico-empleo-perspectiva-latinoamericana-riesgos-la-sustitucion. [6]

Notes

[1] These are the Latin American countries participating in the Survey of Adults Skills (PIAAC) on which OECD estimates of the risk of automation are based.

² The World Bank (2016₍₅₎) and Weller, Gontero and Campbell (2019₍₆₎) estimates are constructed using experts' assessment of the probability that different occupations can be automated and follow the same methodology as Frey and Osborne (2017[33]). Nedelkoska and Quintini (2018[4]), while also departing from Frey and Osborne's analysis, directly explore the task content of individual jobs instead of the average task content within each occupation. Finally, the McKinsey Global Institute (2017[7]) assesses the technical potential for automation through an analysis of the component activities of each occupation. The authors break down about 800 occupations into more than 2 000 activities, and determine the performance capabilities needed for each activity based on the way humans currently perform them. Finally, they further break down each activity into 18 capabilities and assess the technical potential for automation of those capabilities.

³ These developments will be challenging for public budgets and pension systems. Indeed, the falling share of the population at traditionally productive ages means relatively fewer people will pay taxes and social contributions at a time when the rising share of older persons implies that more people will receive pensions and costly health services, etc.

⁴ The old-age dependency ratio is defined as the ratio of those of non-active age (65 and over) to those of active age (20-64) in a given population.

⁵ Also almost half of the regional variation in informality can be attributed to access to good quality higher education (IMF, 2018[23]).

⁶ The Manpower Talent Shortage survey is an annual survey of a subsample of formal firms in the manufacturing sector (https://go.manpowergroup.com/talent-shortage).

⁷ The OECD Skills for Jobs database (OECD, 2017[31]) provides regularly-updated international evidence on skill shortages, surpluses and mismatches, using quantitative information from large-scale datasets (e.g. labour force surveys).

⁸ Chile is the leader producer of copper in the world with a production market share of around 30%. In 2018, this industry represented about 50% of the country's total exports. Recently, there are however signs of a slowdown in this sector as large infrastructure projects are under development.

⁹ See: https://www.oecdskillsforjobsdatabase.org.

3 Coverage and inclusiveness of adult learning in Latin America

This chapter provides an overview of the most salient gaps that affect the inclusiveness of adult learning systems in the Latin America and Caribbean (LAC) region. It also discusses the actions that can be taken to make the access more inclusive and to boost participation of adults in learning activities.

A skilled workforce is a major determinant of economic and labour market performance. Skilled workers have a higher likelihood of being employed, and, at the same time, they tend to be more productive in their jobs.

Latin American and the Caribbean (LAC) countries are characterised by low level of skills, low job quality and pervasive informality (see Chapter 1). Against this backdrop, investments and participation in adult learning become of paramount importance to help adults regularly update, upgrade and acquire entirely new skills to adapt to ever-changing labour markets and societies.

Summary of the main insights

Participation in training in the LAC region stands more than 10 percentage points below the OECD average

- In Latin America, approximately 57% of adults did not participate - and did not want to participate - in adult learning activities (compared to the OECD average of 49%). Participation in adult learning is, however, very heterogeneous. Chile and Peru for instance, show levels of participation that are similar to those of some developed economies such as Japan or Spain and even higher than those of other OECD countries such as Greece, Italy and Turkey. Other LAC countries, instead, lag much behind and too many adults are lacking willingness to participate in training.
- The median number of hours spent on non-formal job related learning per year (an indicator of the intensity of the participation) is significantly lower in LAC countries than on average across OECD countries, suggesting that often times training programmes in Latin America are shorter than across OECD countries.
- Also, the type of training differs between LAC countries and OECD countries. In LAC countries, adults participate more often in informal and less structured training than their peers across OECD countries. On average, for instance, 80% of workers in LAC countries report to learn by doing or from others, keeping their skills up-to-date with new products or services at least once per week but in an informal setting.

Informality represents a major challenge in Latin America

- Evidence shows that informality in LAC countries is linked to weaker participation in training activities: a situation that perpetuates a vicious circle where informal workers do not train and lack of education leads to informality.
- Evidence shows that workers employed without a regular contract are, on average, more than twice less likely to participate in learning activities than their peers who are employed formally. In some countries such as Ecuador, the difference in participation in learning activities between workers with and without an employment contract is staggering; approximately 42 percentage points.

Providing inclusive learning opportunities for all and, particularly to individuals in a region with high levels of inequalities such as Latin America is of paramount importance

- The incidence of adults' participation in training in the region, as across many countries, varies considerably depending on socio-economic background and/or on the employment status of the individual. Much needs to be done to make Adult Learning systems more inclusive. Low skilled individuals, who tend to be in lower-quality jobs, and often in the informal economy, participate less in training. Results show, in fact that one extra year of education increases the likelihood of participating in training by approximately 0.4% across OECD countries and slightly more (approximately 0.5%) and in Latin America.

- Employment status and job quality are also strongly related to the take-up of training. According to the Survey of Adult Skills, a product of the Programme for the International Assessment of Adult Competencies (PIAAC) data, on average in Latin America, the participation rate of the low-wage workers is 26 percentage points lower than that of higher-wages employees. This result is likely to be self-reinforcing, fostering a vicious circle as individuals participating less in training will also struggle the most to find high-quality and well-paying jobs.
- Across LAC countries, the participation of women in learning activities is lower than that of men. Everything else constant, being a woman reduces the likelihood of participating in job-related training by 8% across OECD countries and by almost 19% in LAC countries. This result is driven by the large gap in participation between men and women in Chile, Ecuador and Peru.
- Marital status play a far more important role in LAC countries than across OECD countries when it comes to the decision of participating in training. Being married reduces the likelihood to participate in training. While this probability is small and not significant in OECD countries, it is large and significant (approximately 17%) in LAC countries.
- Perhaps surprisingly, workers with dependent children in LAC countries are significantly more likely to participate in job-related training activities than across OECD countries. One possible explanation can relate to the existence of numerous social protection training programmes implemented in the last two decades targeting vulnerable families (e.g. those where low skilled parents are in precarious jobs) in many LAC countries.
- When focussing on demographic characteristics, the gap in participation between older and younger cohorts is relatively smaller across LAC countries than across many OECD countries. Once accounting for other individual characteristics, for instance, being ten years older is associated with only a 7% lower probability of participating in job-related training by workers in LAC countries.
- In contrast with the majority of OECD countries, LAC countries display a very small gap in participation in adult learning between the unemployed and the employed population (only 8 percentage point differences vs. 17 percentage points across OECD countries). This result can be explained by the fact that most unemployed in LAC countries are young individuals who are also the recipients of the wide majority of public training programmes for adults (*Jovenes* programmes).

Firm size plays a much more important role in Latin America than in the OECD when it comes to engagement in training

- Results show that individuals working in micro and small firms in Latin America are almost twice less likely to receive training than individuals working in firms of similar size across OECD countries. Results seem to suggest that, in Latin America, even more than in other regions, small firms may be facing greater challenges due to their limited capacity to plan, fund and deliver training.
- Despite a widespread lack of interest to participate in training, individuals who have actually participated highly value the usefulness of training.
- Reaching out to adults with information about the returns to training more widely should be a priority for Latin American governments. More effort should be also put in reducing barriers to participation altogether by reducing financial constraints and supporting individuals and families to find time for learning.
- In Latin America, more than 70% of those individuals who actually participated in training found the learning activity very useful, almost 20 percentage points higher than the OECD average. Satisfaction is especially high in Ecuador and Mexico (77% and 79% of individuals who participated respectively) but very high also in Chile and Peru and still above the OECD average.

- Lack of awareness about the effectiveness of training is likely to be at the core of the weak interest of individuals (especially the low skilled) to participate in training. These results seem to suggest that the visibility (i.e. information campaigns, career guidance etc.) and the perception around the usefulness of training activities in Latin America should be strengthened through specific policy interventions aiming at advertising more widely the benefits of learning across individuals who are, too often, lacking incentives to participate in training.
- According to the Survey of Adult Skills (PIAAC) data, the most common barriers to participation in learning activities in Latin America was the cost of training (24.5%), being too busy at work (24%) and childcare or family responsibilities (17%), hinting that lack of time can be an important barrier to participation. Financial constraints are particularly relevant for individuals in Ecuador, Mexico and Peru, while in Chile, being too busy at work is the main reason preventing participation in training.

Participation in adult learning

Despite the importance that training plays in the context of rapidly changing societies and labour markets, evidence for the LAC countries that participated in the Survey of Adult Skills (PIAAC) shows that less than 1 out 3 adults (29%) actually participate in formal or non-formal job-related training.

While low levels of participation in adult learning are a common problem across many countries, participation in training in the region still stands more than 10 percentage points below the OECD average (40%). According to the Survey of Adult Skills (PIAAC) data, however, results are fairly heterogeneous across countries and some LAC economies, Chile and Peru for instance, show levels of participation that are similar to those of developed economies such as Japan or Spain (Figure 3.1) and even higher than those of other OECD countries such as Greece, Italy and Turkey.

One explanation of the relatively high levels of participation in training in some countries in the region can be traced back to the numerous public training programmes offered in those countries (see Chapter 4 for more details). That being said, while head-count participation in some countries may seem to be fairly good, the median number of hours spent on non-formal job related learning per year (an indicator of the intensity of the participation) is significantly lower in LAC countries than the OECD average. This suggests that often times training programmes in Latin America are shorter than across OECD countries.

Figure 3.1. Adults' participation in learning is insufficient in many countries

% of adults participating in formal and non-formal job-related training in the past 12 months

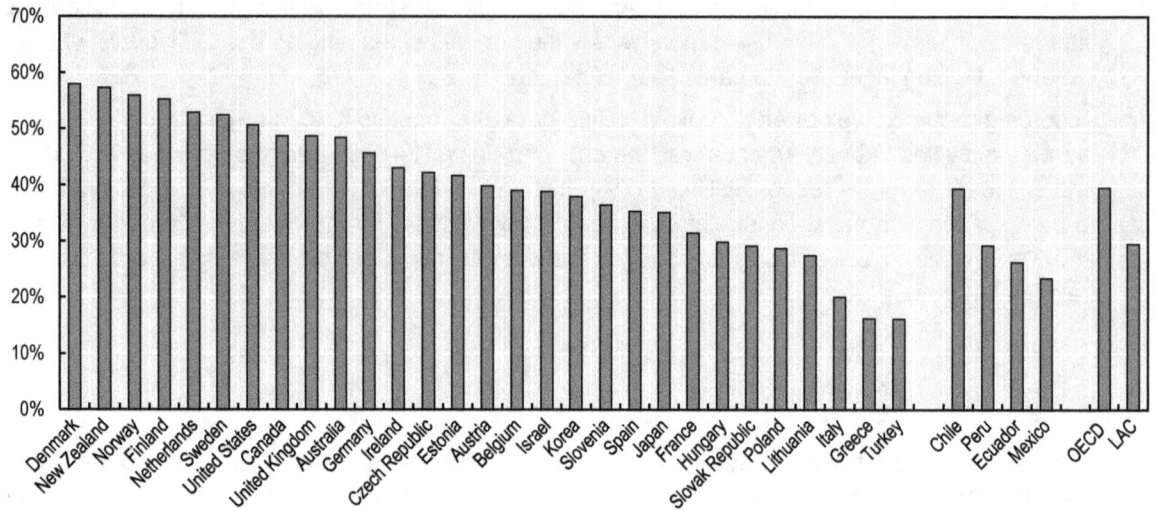

Source: OECD (2019[1]), Priorities for Adult Learning dashboard, http://www.oecd.org/employment/skills-and-work/adult-learning/dashboard.htm.

Other differences between LAC countries and OECD countries relate to the type of training received by adults. In LAC countries, for instance, adults participate more often in informal (Box 3.1) and less structured training than their peers across OECD countries. On average, for instance, 80% of workers in LAC countries report that they learn by doing or from others, keeping their skills up-to-date with new products or services at least once per week (Figure 3.2).

Figure 3.2. Participation in informal learning

% of workers who participate in informal job-related learning.

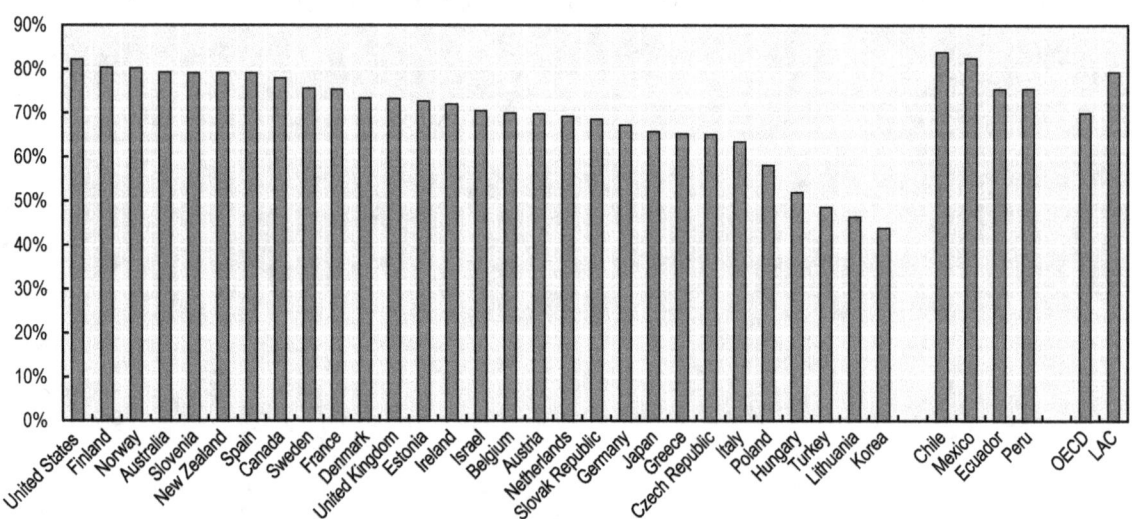

Note: Informal learning is defined as learning from others, learning by doing, or keeping up-to-date with new products or services at least once per week
Source: OECD (2019[1]), Priorities for Adult Learning dashboard, http://www.oecd.org/employment/skills-and-work/adult-learning/dashboard.htm.

> **Box 3.1. Formal, non-formal and informal learning in the Survey of Adults Skills (PIAAC)**
>
> Formal, non-formal and informal learning are measured according to standard definitions, and most of the analysis is restricted to learning that is job-related and that was undertaken in the previous 12 months. In particular:
>
> **Formal learning** is defined as institutionalised, intentional and planned learning that leads to recognised qualifications.
>
> It is important to note that such job-related formal training might have been undertaken in the context of a previous job or to improve outside opportunities. In other words, participation in job-related formal training does not necessarily refers to formal training provided by the current employer with direct application to the current job. Only individuals in paid work who have left the first cycle of formal studies are included in the sample. Hence, formal learning does not refer to initial education but rather to certified courses undertaken by adults while in paid work.
>
> **Non-formal learning** is also institutionalised, intentional and planned, but typically includes shorter or lower-intensity courses, which do not necessarily lead to formal qualifications. This includes on-the-job training, open and distance education, courses and private lessons, seminars and workshops.
>
> Two important facts are worth stressing. Firstly, as it is the case for formal training, the fact that this activity in job-related does not necessarily mean that it is directly related to the current job. Secondly, if the individual took part in more than one non-formal activity, the job-related nature of non-formal training will only refer to the latest activity taken in the last 12 months.
>
> **Informal learning** is defined as intentional learning that is less organised and structured. In the context of this report it includes learning by doing or from colleagues (learning new work-related things from co-workers or supervisors) or keeping up to date with new products and services.
>
> Source: Fialho, P., G. Quintini and M. Vandeweyer (2019[2]), "Returns to different forms of job related training: Factoring in informal learning", *OECD Social, Employment and Migration Working Papers*, No. 231, https://doi.org/10.1787/b21807e9-en.

Chapter 1 already discussed the prevalence of informality in LAC countries and how informal employers may be less keen to provide training to their workers than formal ones. Official statistics on the participation of workers in learning generally struggle to capture the activities of informal workers. New evidence obtained for this report using the Survey of Adult Skills (PIAAC) data on workers declaring to be employed without a formal contract (*de facto*, working informally) show, however, that participation in learning activities differ substantially between formal and informal[1] workers in all the LAC countries for which this information is available (Figure 3.3). In particular, workers employed without a regular contract are, on average, more than twice less likely to participate in learning activities than their peers who are employed formally. In Ecuador, the difference in participation in learning activities between workers with and without an employment contract is staggering; approximately 42 percentage points.

Figure 3.3. Training participation of workers with and without a contract

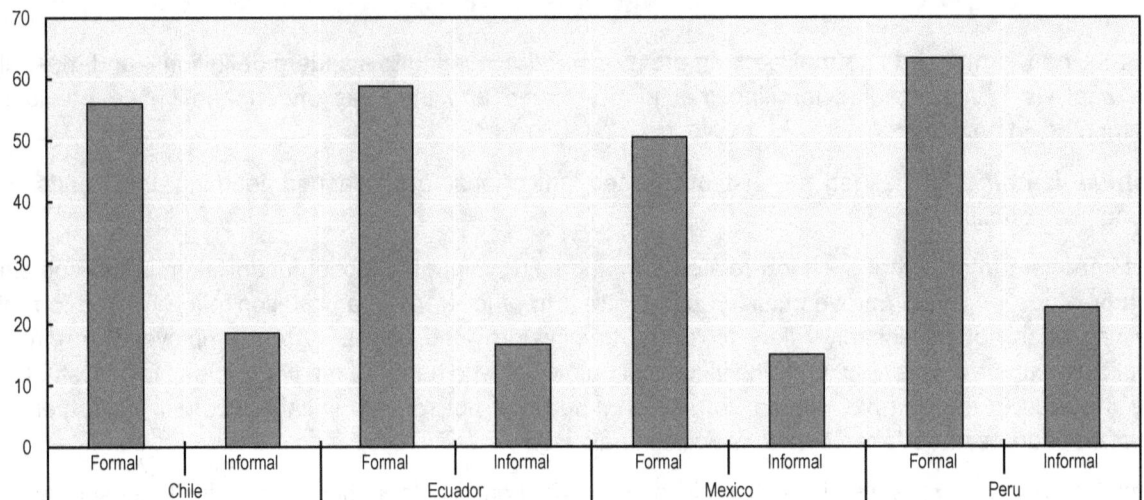

Note: The Survey of Adult Skills (PIAAC) data do not allow to exactly identify informal workers using the common legal or productive definition of informality. Statistics above refer to workers that, despite being employed, reported not to have an employment contract.
Source: OECD calculations using OECD (2017[3]), Survey of Adults Skills (PIAAC) (2012, 2015, 2017) (database), http://www.oecd.org/skills/piaac/.

Inclusiveness of adult learning systems in Latin America

Vulnerable groups generally participate less in training

Ensuring broad-based coverage of adult learning is key to address the challenges of the future of work. Providing inclusive learning opportunities for all - and particularly to individuals in a region with high levels of inequalities such as Latin America - is of paramount importance. However, evidence shows that individuals most exposed to changes in skill needs, those with few and lower qualifications, the long-term unemployed and those at high risk of job automation are least likely to participate in training and are often under-represented in adult learning (OECD, 2019[4]). In Latin America, as across most OECD countries, the incidence of adults' participation in training varies considerably also depending on socio-economic background and/or on the employment status of the individual.

Older workers, women and lower skilled workers in Latin America are, across most other OECD countries, less likely to engage in training. When focussing on demographic characteristics, the gap in participation between older and younger cohorts is, however, relatively smaller across LAC countries than across many OECD countries. Conversely, while the participation of women in learning activities is lower than that of men in both OECD and LAC countries, the gap is more pronounced in favour of men's participation in Latin America, a result that seems to be driven by the relatively large gap in Chile, Ecuador and Peru.

Perhaps not surprisingly, low skilled individuals, who tend to be in lower-quality jobs, and often in the informal economy, participate less in training (see Chapter 1).

Employment status and job-quality (see Chapter 1) are also strongly related to the take-up of training. According to the Survey of Adult Skills (PIAAC) data, on average in Latin America, the participation rate of the low-wage workers[2] is 26 percentage points lower than that of the higher-wages employees. This result is likely to self-reinforce in a vicious circle as individuals participating less in training will also struggle the most to find high-quality and well-paying jobs.

Surprisingly, and in contrast with the majority of OECD countries, LAC countries display a very small gap in participation in adult learning between the unemployed and the employed population (8 percentage-point differences vs. 17 percentage points across OECD countries).

Figure 3.4. Gap in participation, by socio-demographic characteristics

% points difference in participation rate in formal and non-formal job-related training, by: i) age, ii) gender and iii) skill level

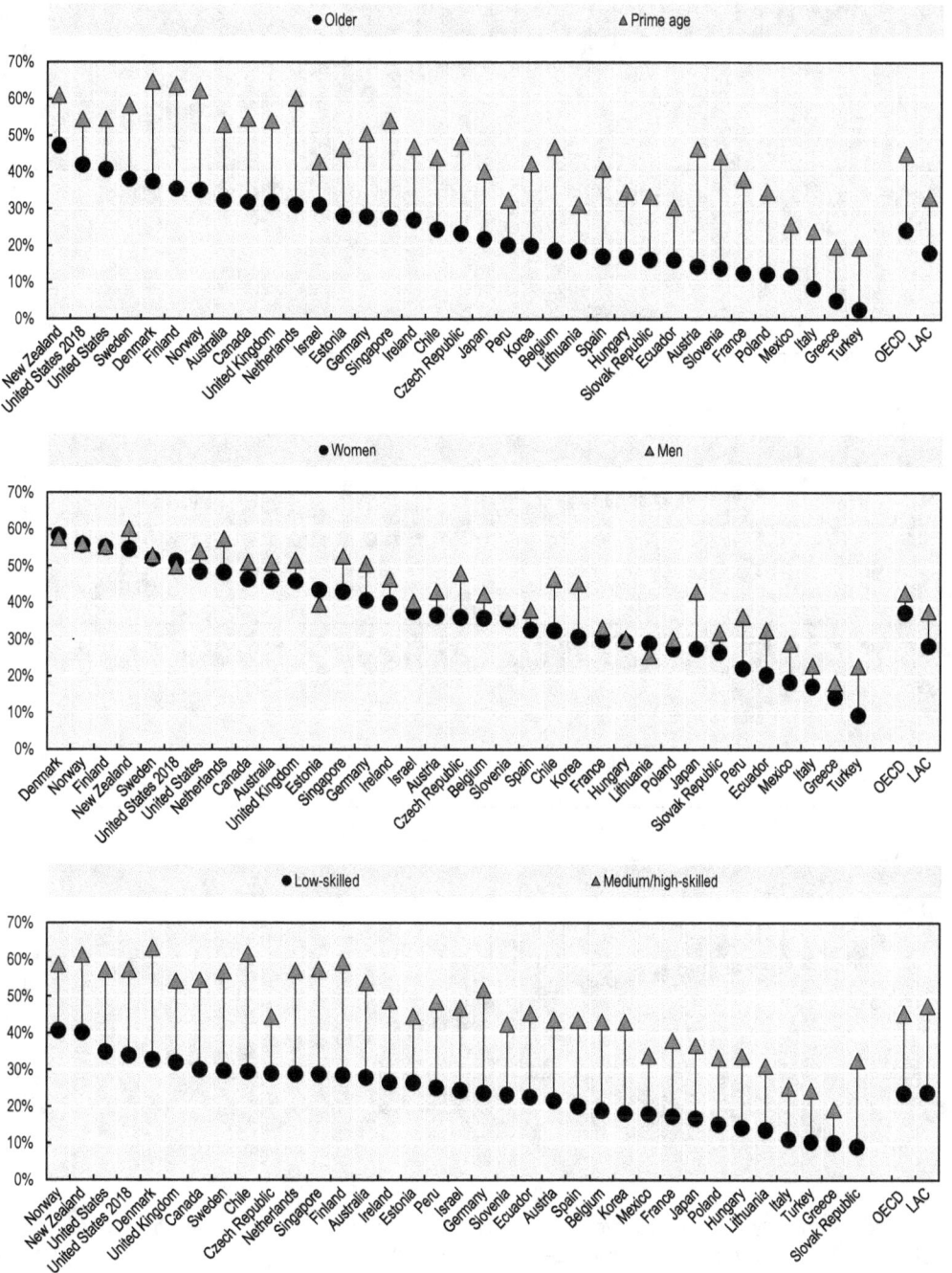

Note: Belgium refers to Flanders only, United Kingdom to England and Northern Ireland; formal and informal job-related education and training.
Source: OECD (2019[1]), Priorities for Adult Learning dashboard, http://www.oecd.org/employment/skills-and-work/adult-learning/dashboard.htm.

Figure 3.5. Gap in participation, by wage and employment characteristics

% points difference in participation rate in formal and non-formal job-related training

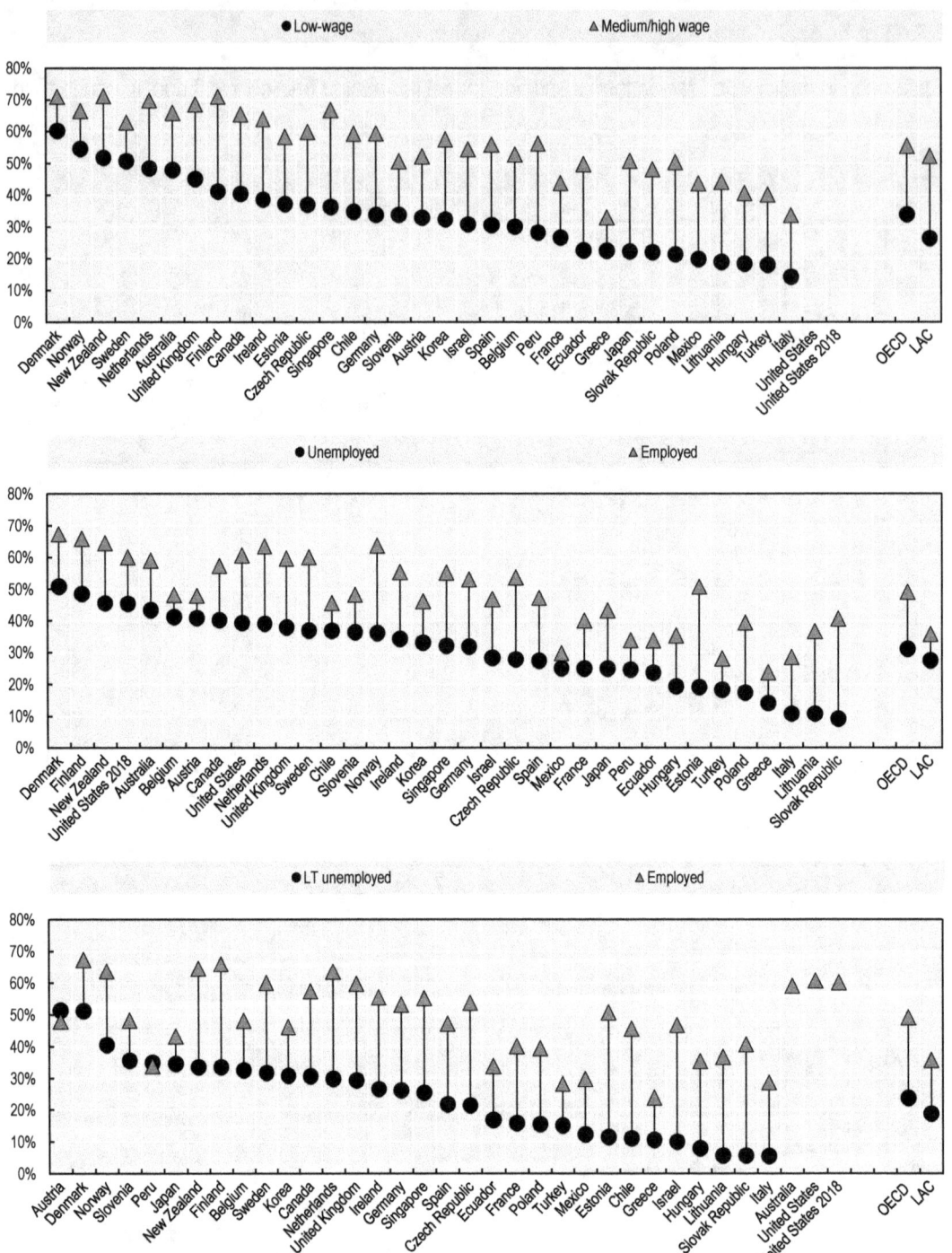

Note: Belgium refers to Flanders only, United Kingdom to England and Northern Ireland; formal and informal job-related education and training.
Source: OECD (2019[1]), Priorities for Adult Learning dashboard, http://www.oecd.org/employment/skills-and-work/adult-learning/dashboard.htm.

This result can be explained by the fact that most unemployed in LAC countries are young individuals[3] who are also the recipients of the wide majority of public training programmes for adults (i.e. *Jovénes* programmes, see Box 3.2).

> ### Box 3.2. Youth Training Programmes in Latin America
>
> Since the 1990s, so-called *Jóvenes* programmes (youth training programmes) have been widely used in Latin America and the Caribbean to improve youth employability. The model, started in Chile, has been replicated in several countries across the region including Argentina, the Bolivarian Republic of Venezuela, Colombia, the Dominican Republic, Panama, Paraguay and Peru. This model targets disadvantaged youth - poor youth, usually from 16 to 24, with low levels of education and experience, unemployed or underemployed - providing them with a combination of vocational training and an internship at a firm in the private sector. Some programmes include socio-emotional skills training. The most generalised version of these programmes lasts in between three to six months only and both employers and participants receive financial incentives such as wage subsidies and daily stipends, respectively. In many cases, training is competitively offered through a public bidding system that ensures quality and fosters the participation of private training centres.
>
> There is evidence that the Jóvenes programmes in Latin America and the Caribbean have had a positive impact on labour insertion and conditions. In particular:
>
> In **Colombia**, *Jóvenes en Acción*, a programme that involved three months of classroom training and three months of apprenticeship in a private company. A randomised-controlled trial found the programme increased the probability of employment and wages for participants, especially for women (Attanasio, Kugler and Meghir, 2011[5]). Additionally, the gains have been found to be long-lasting. The programme had also a positive and significant effect of working in the formal sector (Attanasio et al., 2015[6]).
>
> In **Argentina**, *Entra21*, a programme providing technical and life-skills training and internship with private sector employers. An experimental evaluation of the programme found that participants increased their probability of working in formal employment and also exhibited earnings about 40% higher than those in the control group (Alzua, Cruces and Lopez, 2016[7]).
>
> In the **Dominican Republic**, *Juventud y Empleo*, is a training programme focused on improving vocational skills followed by a short internship in a private-sector firm. A randomised evaluation found positive effect on wages but not on employment, one year after training (Card et al., 2011[8]). A more recent study estimated the long-term effects found that a widening of the formal employability gap between treatment and control groups (Ibarraran et al., 2015[9]).
>
> In **Chile**, *Chile Jóven*, a programme targeted at a group of urban youth considered to be "at risk" of social exclusion. The training was offered in two successive stages: a stage of working training lectures conducted by a training institution and a stage involving on the-job-learning in firm (an internship for a period of 3-6 months). Evaluations of this programme suggest that employment effects range from modest to meaningful –increasing the employment rate up to 5 percentage points with impact of 6 to 12 percentage points in the employment rate. In most cases results show a larger and significant impact on job quality, measured by getting a formal job, having a contract and/or receiving health insurance as a benefit (González-Velosa, Ripani and Rosas-Shady, 2012[10]).
>
> Source: Busso, M. et al (2017[11]), *Learning Better: Public Policy for Skills Development*, http://dx.doi.org/10.18235/0000799; J-PAL (2017[12]), *J-PAL Skills for Youth Program Review Paper*.

The drivers of training participation in Latin America and across OECD countries

According to data from the Survey of Adult Skills (PIAAC), only 41% of adults in the surveyed OECD countries participate in formal or non-formal job-related training in a given year. Out of the remaining 59% of adults who did not participate in training, up to 49% declared not to be interested in doing so, fundamentally being disengaged or not motivated.

Disentangling the different drivers associated to the lack of participation in adult learning in LAC is of key importance to provide insights to policy makers on how to make their adult learning systems more effective and promote a culture of learning. Econometric analysis carried out for this report focuses on the various potential drivers of participation in training and confirms the descriptive statistics presented above while it also sheds light on some interesting differences between OECD and LAC countries.

First, the analysis corroborates the existence of a relationship between likelihood of participation in training and age, gender as well as years of education. Importantly, those relationships maintain statistical significance despite the inclusion of a large set of individual, job and employer characteristics controls in the regression. For instance, when looking at demographic characteristics, regression results show that holding everything else constant, being ten years older is associated with a 10% lower probability of participating in job-related training across OECD countries and 7% in LAC countries.

Education also plays an important role in explaining participation in training. Results show, in fact that one extra year of education increases the likelihood of participating in training by approximately 0.4% across OECD countries and slightly more (approximately 0.5%) in Latin America.

Regression analysis also shows that, holding other individual characteristics constant, gender and marital status play a far more important role in LAC countries than across OECD countries when it comes to the decision of participating in training. Notably, women in Latin America are much less likely to participate in training than men. Everything else constant, being a woman reduces the likelihood of participating in job-related training by 8% across OECD countries and by almost 19% in LAC countries. Being married also reduces the likelihood to participate in training, but while this probability is small and not significant across OECD countries, it is large and significant (approximately 17%) in LAC countries.

Interestingly, workers with dependent children in LAC countries are significantly more likely to participate in job-related training activities than across OECD countries. One possible explanation can relate to the existence of numerous social protection training programmes implemented in the last two decades targeting vulnerable families in many LAC countries (see Chapter 4).

Interestingly, and partly linked to the result highlighting the higher propensity of skilled workers to participate in training, regression analysis also shows that individuals employed in relatively more complex jobs (i.e. jobs requiring three or more years of experience) are twice more likely to engage in training activities in Latin America countries than across OECD countries. Workers in part-time jobs are also less likely to engage in learning activities across OECD countries, as well as in LAC countries.

Finally, employers and firms' characteristics also matter a great deal for training participation. The size of the firm, for instance, plays a much more marked role in Latin America than across OECD countries. In particular, results show that individuals working in micro-small firms in Latin America are almost twice less likely to receive any training than individuals working in firms of similar size across OECD countries. Results seem to suggest that, in Latin America, even more than in other regions, small firms may be facing greater challenges due to their more limited capacity to plan, fund and deliver training.

Given that much learning takes place in the workplace, the engagement of employers in the design, implementation and financing of skill development opportunities is key to the success of adult learning systems. This result, coupled with the fact that small and micro firms are the vast majority of firms in LAC countries poses the fundamental challenge of finding policy mechanisms to spur a more effective engagement of small employers in the delivery of adult learning.

Table 3.1. Likelihood of training participation, by individual, job and firm characteristics

Probit regressions marginal effects

	(1)	(2)	(3)
Dependent variable:	Formal or non-formal job-related adult learning		
	Full sample	OECD	LAC
Female	-0.066***	-0.082***	-0.186***
Age	-0.012***	-0.010***	-0.007**
Married	-0.013	-0.006	-0.168***
With dependent children	0.047*	0.035	0.235***
Not a native speaker	-0.147***	-0.158***	-0.290**
Education in years	0.032***	0.038***	0.046***
Micro-small firm (max 50 employees)	-0.372***	-0.343***	-0.586***
Medium size firm (51-250 employees)	-0.143***	-0.121***	-0.253***
Employer grew in size	0.157***	0.129***	0.117*
Private sector	-0.092***	-0.141***	-0.110
Part time	-0.198***	-0.198***	-0.163**
Atypical contract	-0.008	-0.008	-0.072
Supervising activity	0.246***	0.235***	0.295***
Dissatisfied with current job	-0.047	-0.069*	-0.053
Informal worker	-0.295***	-0.267***	-0.305***
Tenure in current job (years)	0.003**	0.002*	-0.002
High complexity job	0.320***	0.290***	0.390***
Medium complexity job	0.201***	0.203***	0.303***
Experience required: 3+ years	0.183***	0.196***	0.378***
Experience required: 7months to 2 years	0.111***	0.129***	0.133**
Proficiency score for numeracy	0.002***	0.001***	-0.001
Occupation FE	yes	yes	yes
Industry FE	yes	yes	yes
Country FE	yes	yes	yes
Observations	92 692	83 200	7 230
Pseudo R2	0.173	0.156	0.211

Note: The regression includes country, occupation (1-digit) and industry (1-digit) dummies. Marginal effects for categorical variables refer to a discrete change from the base level. Proficiency in literacy is measured on a 500-point scale but is divided by 10 for presentational purposes. Significance levels as follows: * $p < .1$, ** $p < .05$, *** $p < .01$.
Source: OECD calculations based on OECD (2017[3]), Survey of Adults Skills (PIAAC) (2012, 2015, 2017) (database), http://www.oecd.org/skills/piaac/.

Barriers to training participation in Latin America

In a world that is rapidly changing, those who do not engage in lifelong and adult learning are likely to suffer poor labour market outcomes and the risk of being left behind. Against this backdrop, however, too many adults still do not engage in training and show little interest in doing so altogether.

Results from the OECD Survey of Adults Skills (PIAAC) show that in LAC countries for which information is available, 57% of adults did not participate and did not want to participate in adult learning activities (compared to the already very high OECD average of 49%).

Despite the widespread lack of interest to participate in training, the perceived usefulness of training among individuals who have actually participated is considerably high. In Latin America, according to Survey of Adult Skills (PIAAC) data, with more than 70% of those individuals who participated in training found the learning activity very useful, almost 20 percentage points higher than the OECD average. Satisfaction is especially high in Ecuador and Mexico (77% and 79% of individuals who participated respectively) but very high also in Chile and Peru and still above the OECD average.[4]

Figure 3.6. Perceptions towards training usefulness

% of participants for whom at least one job-related adult learning activity was "very useful" for the job

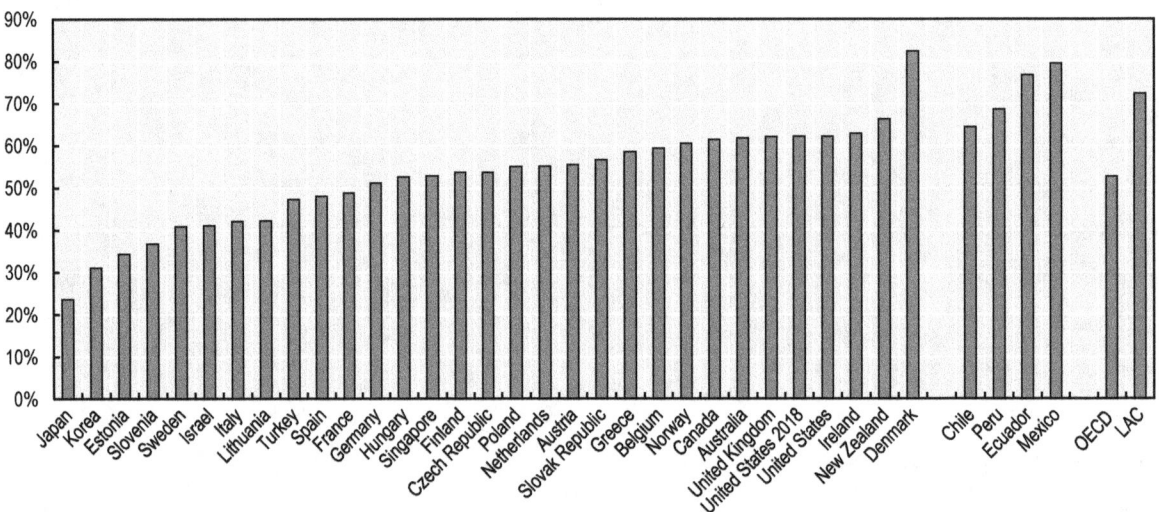

Source: OECD calculations based on OECD (2017[3]), Survey of Adults Skills (PIAAC) (2012, 2015, 2017) (database), http://www.oecd.org/skills/piaac/.

Providing information and guidance can spur stronger participation in training

Lack of awareness about the effectiveness of training is likely to be at the core of the weak interest of individuals (especially the low skilled) in participating in training. These results seem to suggest that the visibility (i.e. information campaigns, career guidance, etc.) and the perception around the usefulness of training activities in Latin America should be strengthened through specific policy interventions aiming at advertising more widely the benefits of learning across individuals who are, too often, lacking incentives to participate in training.

Reaching out to the people excluded from adult learning provisions and raising awareness on the benefits of learning as well as providing high-quality information, advice and guidance is an important step to engage them proactively in training.

Public awareness campaigns may come in many forms. For instance, outreach through the workplace can be effective, particularly in engaging low skilled adults. In this context, trade unions can act as a bridge functioning between employers and employees with low skills who might be hesitant or unable to express their training needs (Stuart et al., 2016[13]; Parker, 2007[14]). In the United Kingdom, for instance, *Unionlearn*, supports workers in acquiring skills and qualifications to improve employability by using Union Learning Representatives (ULRs) to reach out to workers and help them identify their needs and arrange learning opportunities.

A community-based approach can also operate as a bridge between low-skilled adults and training opportunities. In Argentina, for example, community leaders share information on available training courses under the *Hacemos Futuro* programme. This programme aims at supporting school dropouts in gaining primary and secondary qualifications and providing access to vocational training. Potential participants receive the information via mobile phone and bring together people in their community to pass the information (OECD, 2019[4]). This is particularly relevant in a context with low digitalisation and internet connectivity, as it can often be the case in many LAC countries or, for instance, in rural areas (see Chapter 3).

Career guidance is another tool that allows individuals to assess one's skill set and plan her/his skills development plan as well as the training programmes that are most appropriate to achieve the result. It is, however, very difficult to get career guidance right and in many countries these activities are under-funded and non-effective. In order for career guidance to be effective, this needs to be based on timely labour market information and on the outputs of skill assessment and anticipation exercises (see Chapter 3).

Financial constraints are significant barriers to participation in training, but well-designed financial incentives could help overcome these obstacles

Among those who did not engage in training, a non-negligible share of adults (14%) wanted to participate but were not able due to a variety of obstacles. According to the Survey of Adult Skills (PIAAC) data, the most common barriers to participation in learning activities in Latin America were financial barriers (the cost of training, 24.5%), being too busy at work (24%) and childcare or family responsibilities (17%). Financial constraints are particularly relevant for Ecuador, Mexico and Peru, while in Chile, being too busy at work is the main reason preventing participation in training (Figure 3.7).

Figure 3.7. Reasons preventing participation in (more) formal and/or non-formal education

% of adults who wanted to participate in (more) training but did not

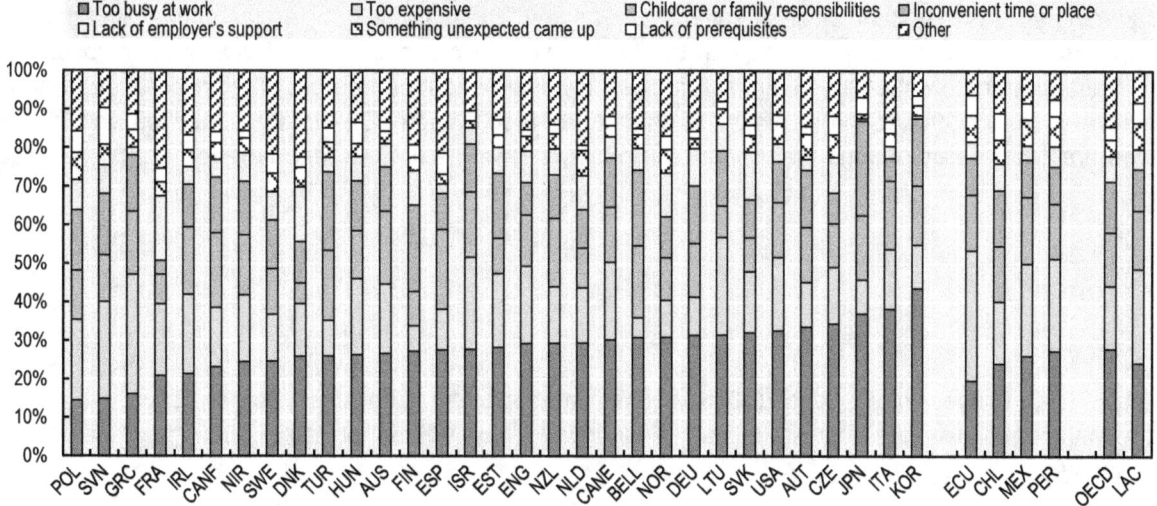

Source: OECD (2017[3]), Survey of Adult Skills (PIAAC) (2012, 2015, 2017) (database), http://www.oecd.org/skills/piaac/.

Financial constraints seem to be particularly important in Latin America in preventing individuals from participating in training. This issue is particularly severe for low-skilled individuals, who often end up holding low-quality informal jobs with limited opportunities for employer-sponsored training or alternate between work and periods of unemployment.

Many workers may also feel disengaged as there is substantial uncertainty about whether participating in training will actually lead to positive labour market returns or have a clear impact on their career progression.[5]

Designing policy incentives aimed at strengthening the linkages between labour market and career progression and the participation in training (making the former conditional on the latter, for instance) could go a long way in providing robust incentives to individuals to engage in learning and address financial constraints hindering participation. More training, in turn, would lead to obvious benefits spreading to firms and employers who could count on a more skilled workforce able to increase productivity and adopt new technologies.

Targeted financial incentives may help adult learning systems becoming more equitable and preventing underinvestment. Many OECD countries have implemented measures such as training vouchers, allowances, wage and training subsidies, tax incentives and individualised learning account schemes to encourage training participation (OECD, 2017$_{[15]}$).

Lack of time is a major obstacle to participate in training

Another key obstacle for adult participation in training that emerged from analysis with the Survey of Adult Skills (PIAAC) data is the lack of time, for both family and work-related reasons. Being too busy at work and childcare or family responsibilities were mentioned to be important barriers in 24 and 17% of the cases respectively. The delivery of flexible adult learning courses can greatly help overcome some of these barriers. Modular training, which divide a learning programme into self-contained modules, can allow adults to learn at their own pace and reduce constraints related to lack of time to follow the courses. A good example of a modular learning programme is the *Modelo Educación oara la Vida y el Trabajo - MEVyT* (Model for Life and Work Programme), in Mexico. MEVyT allows adults to obtain qualifications through different modules at initial, intermediate (primary education) and advanced (lower secondary education) level. The programme allows individuals to choose their own learning programme and gives them choice on the learning mode (i.e. if studying on their own or in group setting in community learning centres, on line or in a mobile learning space) (OECD, 2019$_{[4]}$).

Digital and online training programmes (e.g. e-learning) can also help enhance flexibility in learning, broadening access to training while keeping the costs low. These training, however, come with important drawbacks that are especially important in the LAC region. In particular, use of digital technologies can limit, the access of low-skilled and digital illiterate individuals and it can be out of reach for those who do not have access to broadband or digital infrastructures (see Chapter 3). Finally, education and training leaves are other policy options that enhance flexibility allowing adults to take time for learning (OECD, 2019$_{[4]}$).

References

Alzua, M., G. Cruces and C. Lopez (2016), "Long-run effects of youth training programs: experimental evidence from Argentina.", *Economic Inquiry*, Vol. 54, pp. 1839-1859, https://doi.org/10.1111/ecin.12348. [7]

Attanasio, O. et al. (2015), "Long term impacts of vouchers for vocational training: Experimental evidence for Colombia", *NBER Working Paper Series*, No. 21390, National Bureau of Economic Research, Cambridge MA, http://dx.doi.org/10.3386/w21390. [6]

Attanasio, O., A. Kugler and C. Meghir (2011), "Subsidizing vocational training for disadvantaged youth in Colombia: Evidence from a randomized trial", *American Economic Journal: Applied Economics*, Vol. 33/3, pp. 188-220, http://dx.doi.org/10.1257/app.3.3.188. [5]

Busso, M. et al. (2017), *Learning Better: Public Policy for Skills Development*, Inter-American Development Bank, Washington, D.C, http://dx.doi.org/10.18235/0000799. [11]

Card, D. et al. (2011), "The labor market impacts of youth training in the Dominican Republic", *Journal of Labor Economics*, Vol. 29/2, pp. 267-300. [8]

Fialho, P., G. Quintini and M. Vandeweyer (2019), "Returns to different forms of job related training: Factoring in informal learning", *OECD Social, Employment and Migration Working Papers*, No. 231, https://doi.org/10.1787/b21807e9-en. [2]

González-Velosa, C., L. Ripani and D. Rosas-Shady (2012), *How Can Job Opportunities for Young People in Latin America be Improved?*, Inter-American Development Bank, Washington D.C., https://publications.iadb.org/publications/english/document/How-Can-Job-Opportunities-for-Young-People-in-Latin-America-be-Improved.pdf. [10]

Ibarraran, P. et al. (2015), "Experimental Evidence on the Long-Term Impacts of a Youth Training Program", *IZA Discussion Paper Series*, No. 9136., IZA. [9]

J-PAL (2017), *J-PAL Skills for Youth Program Review Paper*, Abdul Latif Jameel Poverty Action Lab, Cambridge, MA. [12]

OECD (2019), *Getting Skills Right: Future-Ready Adult Learning Systems*, Getting Skills Right, OECD Publishing, Paris, https://dx.doi.org/10.1787/9789264311756-en. [4]

OECD (2019), *Priorities for Adult Learning dashboard*, http://www.oecd.org/employment/skills-and-work/adult-learning/dashboard.htm. [1]

OECD (2017), *Getting Skills Right: Skills for Jobs Indicators*, Getting Skills Right, OECD Publishing, Paris, https://dx.doi.org/10.1787/9789264277878-en. [15]

OECD (2017), *Survey of Adults Skills (PIAAC) (2012, 2015, 2017)*, (database), http://www.oecd.org/skills/piaac/. [3]

OECD/CAF/UN ECLAC (2016), *Latin American Economic Outlook 2017: Youth, Skills and Entrepreneurship*, OECD Publishing, Paris, https://dx.doi.org/10.1787/leo-2017-en. [16]

Parker, J. (2007), *Policy Brief Workplace Education: Twenty State Perspectives*, National Commission on Adult Literacy, http://www.caalusa.org/content/parkerpolicybrief.pdf. [14]

Stuart, M. et al. (2016), *Evaluation of the Union Learning Fund Rounds 15-16 and Support Role of Unionlearn*, University of Leeds, https://www.unionlearn.org.uk/sites/default/files/publication/ULF%20Eval%201516%20FINAL%20REPORT.pdf. [13]

Notes

[1] While the Survey of Adult Skills (PIAAC) data do not allow to exactly identify informal workers using the common legal or productive definition of informality, they allow to identify workers that, despite being employed, do not have a contract.

[2] Low wage workers are those who earn less than two-thirds of median wages.

[3] Unemployment rates are almost three times higher for youth aged 15-29 (11.2%) than for adults aged 30-64 (3.7%) in all countries in Latin America and the Caribbean (OECD/CAF/UN ECLAC, 2016[16]).

[4] These results should, however, taken with caution as self-reported satisfaction may, in some cases, respond to cultural and subjective biases.

[5] Results from probit regression analysis run on the probability of non-participating in training and not wanting to participate confirm findings in the literature that those who would benefit the most from training – i.e. the least skilled workers, most vulnerable workers – tend not to participate (and to be under-represented). These results are not shown but available upon request.

4 Policies to spur adult learning in Latin America: Challenges and solutions

This chapter provides an overview of the challenges to policy makers, employers and individuals in spurring and designing effective adult learning systems in Latin America. The chapter looks, in particular, at the role of government, employers and individuals in the governance and financing of adult learning. It discusses the limits of existing approaches and provides examples of international best practices to improve the co-ordination and coherence across all actors of the adult learning system.

Lifelong learning policies aim to allow workers, particularly the most vulnerable, to acquire and maintain relevant skills. Unfortunately, however, most countries in Latin America and the Caribbean (LAC) lack a lifelong learning system with a clear national regulatory framework and a national strategy (OECD, 2018[1]; OECD, 2019[2]).

Governments are increasingly facing tight budget constraints making it difficult for countries to ensure financial support to training activities. Striking the right balance between public and private incentives to steer and foster adult learning and diversifying the sources of funding, by calling for all stakeholders, including the government itself, employers and individual workers, to contribute equitably to lifelong learning activities, could mitigate this problem.

Governments are, therefore, called upon to create effective mechanisms in which both the private and public sector play a joint role (Busso et al., 2017[3]). This is particularly relevant in Latin America, where many workers in the workforce need support to find high-quality formal jobs and adapt to the changing skill demands of the labour market.

Summary of the main insights

On average, LAC countries spend almost half the OECD average on active labour market policies (ALMPs). Boosting support to ALMPs is key to provide individuals with high-quality training opportunities

- With the exception of Colombia and Chile, public spending for training measures in LAC countries is well below the OECD average. For instance, in Argentina, spending in training is roughly half that of the OECD average, and in Brazil and Mexico, funding allocated to training has decreased considerably in recent years to very low levels.

One way to support training in Latin America has been to subsidise its supply through the creation of National Training Institutes (NTI). Their action, however, could be strengthened, as the take up of the training offer is low

- NTIs, national agencies tasked to supply and oversee training, are common across LAC countries. These are financed with a specific tax on the payroll of formal workers that ranges from 0.25% (Uruguay) to 2% (Colombia) but even when these investments are sizable, the effectiveness of their action could be strengthened.
- NTIs' training reaches only a small fraction of employed workers. Evidence is that, in the region, less than 15% of employed workers accessed training provided by NTIs – the only exception is Colombia where up to 24% of workers were involved.
- In addition, evidence based on a survey of formal firms in the Bahamas, Colombia, Honduras, Panama and Uruguay, shows that, on average, less than 12% of firms makes use of public resources to finance their training initiatives, and when used, this funding generally goes to large firms.

Governments in Latin America are making important steps towards designing training interventions that respond to the skill needs of connected and digital labour markets

- In Mexico, 32 Digital Inclusion Centres (Puntos Mexico Conectado – Centros de Inclusión Digital) have been set up across the country, providing basic digital skills programmes. Peru passed the National Digital Literacy Plan to train individuals in information and communication technologies (ICT) skills, the use of computer tools as well as mobile devices. Around 107 online courses were made available also to teachers as part of the Educate Peru Programme with emphasis on developing digital skills to incorporate ICT use in the classroom. Brazil and Costa Rica have been devoting resources to finance the development of ICT skills in universities and graduate courses.

As digital technologies spread across the region, online learning offers a significant opportunity to leverage broadband networks to spread knowledge in a cost-effective way

- Massive Open Online Courses (MOOCs), academic courses offered on line often provided at no cost, aim at large-scale interactive participation from around the world can be powerful tools to spur learning in the region. These, however, face challenges of implementation and take up. According to the Survey of Adult Skills, a product of the Programme for the International Assessment of Adult Competencies (PIAAC), individuals who are more likely to participate in open education in Latin America, as across OECD countries more broadly, are mainly young, educated and skilled workers. This situation potentially leaves out the most vulnerable and the low-skilled most in need of receiving training. Efforts need to be put in reinforcing the ICT skills of disadvantaged groups and to create suitable options for them to use digital technologies for learning.
- MOOCs and online courses do not usually lead to a certification, a qualification or a title that can be used in the labour market to signal one's credentials and skills. Micro-credentials are mostly unregulated and the validation of contents and of quality varies very much across the spectrum of available training options. This poses several challenges as the lack of a certification framework hinders the acceptance of MOOCs and online courses and their use as a signal for skills in the labour market.

The content of adult learning programmes in LAC countries needs to align with current (and future) skills needs in the labour market

- Data collection infrastructures should be developed to timely analyse labour market needs and for this information to feed into curricula revision. Skill Assessment and Anticipation (SAA) exercises are, sometimes, not well-aligned with the potential policy uses. For instance, the way skills are defined is not always useful for policy-making, providing an output that the policy maker does not understand and whose results are insufficiently disaggregated at the regional, sub-regional or sectoral levels for the policy makers to be able to use them.

Some countries in Latin America have implemented good initiatives to improve labour market and skills information to improve matching of skills demand and supply

- In Chile, the Public Employment Service uses information on labour demand, collected through interviews, surveys and roundtables, to align their training offer with labour market needs. In addition, the government runs an online portal called the National Employment Exchange (BNE), a free site where companies publish job offers and workers can submit CVs for consideration.
- In the Dominican Republic, the Ministry of Labour created a job portal that matches employers with potential workers. Candidates can register their information and apply to jobs. In September 2015, 11 000 businesses were listed on the platform and nearly 42 000 jobs posted.
- In Brazil, as part of the Pronatec programme, different ministries can submit requests to the Ministry of Education for creating specific training programmes that correspond to the identified skill needs. The Ministry of Education centralises these requests and co-ordinates the opening of funded training programmes with public and private training providers.

The direct involvement of employers in supporting training in LAC countries is substantial

- Some 30% to 50% of LAC firms in the manufacturing sector offered training through short, structured courses focusing on specific job-related skills. In addition, on average across LAC countries participating in the OECD Survey of Adult Skills (PIAAC), 63% of workers who participated in training report to have received funding from her/his employers for at least one learning activities. Mexico shows the largest share of workers receiving support from employers, above 80%. In Ecuador, instead, this is the lowest (around 60%) pointing to the fact that while many firms in the country engage in training (more than 73% of the total), the support provided by employers covers a relatively smaller share of their employees.
- The participation in training activities of firms of different sizes varies quite a lot. In particular, SMEs participate in training activities much less than larger firms in the region. Little can be said about the engagement of informal firms in training, though these represent the majority of businesses in LAC countries.
- Large variations in the number of people involved in training is recorded across countries. Evidence shows that firms in Latin America train between 49% (in Chile) and 78 % (in Ecuador) of their workers, though no information is available about the duration of the training nor on the training provided by informal firms (if any).

The size and the managerial quality of LAC firms matter a lot when explaining participation in training

- In Latin America, smaller firms are less likely to provide training to workers than larger firms. Data from the Survey of Adult Skills (PIAAC) show that only 40% of workers in SMEs participated in training, compared to 69% workers in larger firms. While a similar pattern can be found in all other countries participating in the OECD Survey of Adult Skills (PIAAC), in Latin America the gap in training provision between small and large firms is almost twice as high (approx. 30%) as the OECD average (17%). This gap, that in Mexico and Ecuador is even greater than 30%, is particularly worrying and represents a key challenge for Latin America, considering that SMEs account for more than 80% of employment and more than 90% of firms in Latin America.

More should be done to provide incentives to SMEs to adopt good managerial practices and leverage their human capital

- Recent estimates show that a 1% increase in the share of high-skilled workers could lead, on average, up to a 0.7% increase in productivity in large firms but no effect is observed for smaller firms. Part of the difference between how large and small firms are able to benefit from skilled workers could be explained by the differences in managerial skills across firms of different sizes.
- Evidence from the World Management Survey shows that managerial quality in LAC countries stands below that of the OECD average and that firms are more poorly run than across OECD countries. The performance is especially low in countries such as Brazil and Colombia, while firms in Mexico reach OECD-average standards. This suggests that relatively few managers in the region follow the best management practices and many would benefit from receiving training in this area.

A range of market failures and barriers (i.e. lack of information, capacity and/or resources) lead to sub-optimal engagement in training, particularly in the case of SMEs

- Creating employer networks can be a solution to the lack of managerial skills in SMEs as these often provide leadership and management skills programmes, in addition to their role as facilitators of knowledge exchange and capacity building. Networks of employers have also the key advantage of pooling the resources of smaller actors together, creating a critical mass and economies of scale that SMEs can leverage to their own advantage.

Well-designed financial incentives steered by government intervention can be a useful tool to boost incentives but potential deadweight losses need to be minimised

- The design of financial incentives needs to consider the institutional context as well as the specific objectives that such policy intervention is meant to achieve. In the case of skill development policies, before introducing any intervention, the policy maker should carefully assess the reasons for any apparent under-investment in training and the best way to create (or restore) adequate incentives with minimum intervention.
- In addition, the efficacy of financial incentives depends on a range of framework conditions being in place in the country. For instance, while providing financial support to firms may be desirable to reduce the cost associated to their participation in training, doing so without setting up a solid skills information system that supports employers in making informed decisions on the choice of education providers or on the skills to be developed, may lead to considerable misuse of resources.
- Targeting financial incentives at employers rather than at individuals has the advantage that training is more likely to meet the specific needs of the firms and, therefore, to fill concrete gaps in labour market needs. One drawback, however, is that, by providing direct and unconditional support to employers through cash transfers, the government risks not being able to reach disadvantaged and vulnerable workers as employers have weaker incentives to provide training to those groups. Intermediate solutions can be found so that the financial incentives are designed to reach employers under the condition that these provide training also to disadvantaged workers. Funds can also be made conditional on supplying training to the unemployed to ensure their re-inclusion in the labour market.

Public provided training in Latin America

Public spending in training is generally low in Latin America

On average, LAC countries spend almost half than the average OECD country on active labour market policies (ALMPs) (Figure 4.1, Panel A). Wide differences exist between OECD and LAC countries when it comes to the focus, scope and configuration of ALMPs policies owing to their particular priorities (e.g. different social challenges) and to the different social and labour market challenges.

In terms of the operation of the labour market, two main differences have affected the functioning of Active Labour Market Policies (ALMPs). First, unlike in OECD countries, labour markets in emerging and developing countries are typically characterised by a growing labour force, low levels of unemployment (albeit high levels of underemployment and low job quality) and higher rates of informal employment (see Chapter 1). Second, labour market and social institutions in LAC countries often have relatively weak capacity to implement programmes compared with those in OECD countries. In emerging market economies such as Colombia, Costa Rica and Mexico the capacity of the public sector is weak, both in terms of human and financial resources, and corruption remains widespread and the rule of law weak (Kaufmann, Kraay and Zoido-Lobaton, 1999[4]). These factors hinder the effective implementation of policies. This may limit the effectiveness of government programmes in general, including that of ALMPs, which usually require large public implementation capacity (ILO, 2016[5]).

Among ALMPs, spending on training generally represents an important component of policy strategies that aim to improve the employability of individuals and thus enhance their future career paths (e.g. higher earnings or improved job quality) with positive aggregate spillover effects (e.g. increased productivity). Publicly provided training often targets disadvantaged individuals – including youth, women, disabled or older workers.

In OECD countries, training represents the main item of expenditure within ALMPs and expenditures are commonly targeted both to on-the-job and/or off-the-job training. The latter is usually directed at unemployed individuals but, in some cases, also used for the employed[1] and training can be part of a broader strategy or comprised within a public works programme and include some form of income support (see Box 4.1 on a welfare programme boosting employment and job quality in Peru). One major difference between LAC countries and OECD countries is that, in the former, training is often of rather short duration and focused on the acquisition of basic skills (ILO, 2016[5]).

Figure 4.1. Spending on active labour market policies is below the OECD average

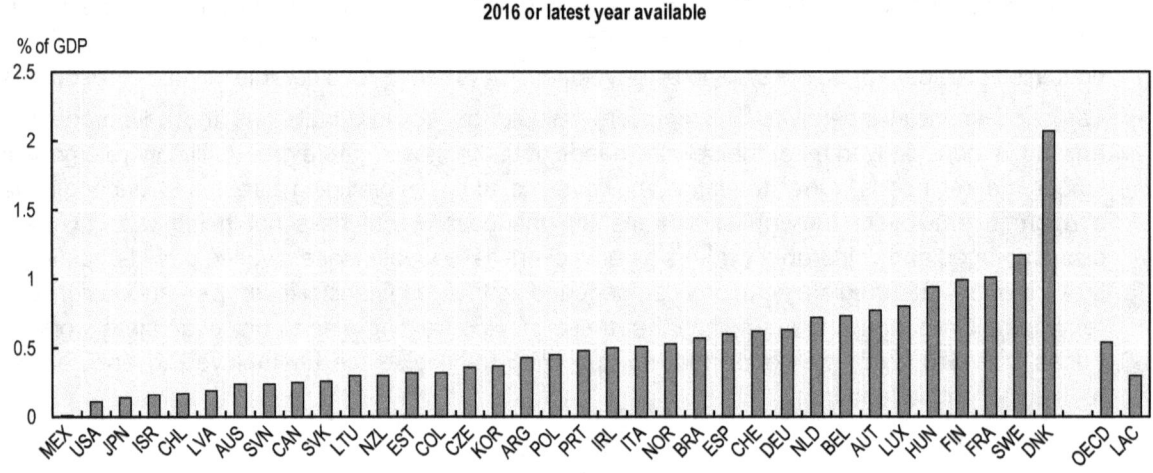

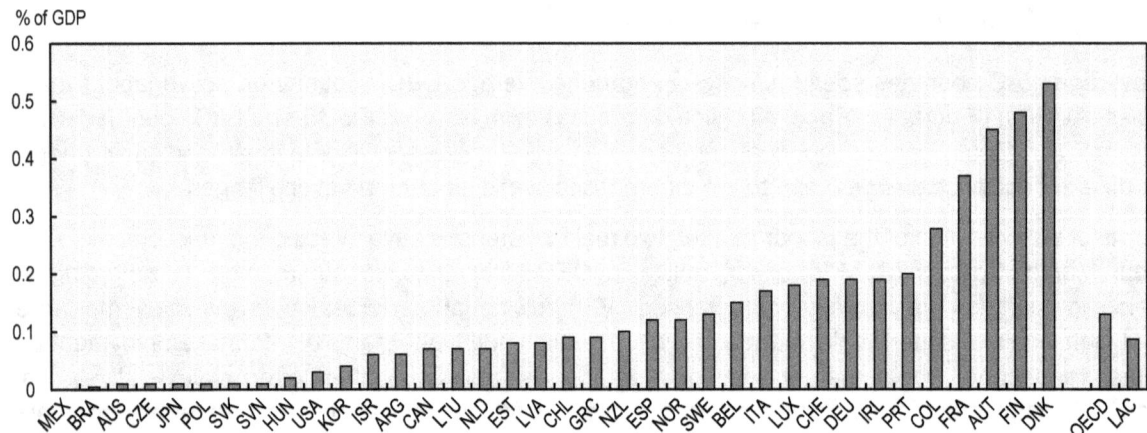

Source: OECD (2019[6]), "Public expenditure and participant stocks related to active labour market policies", *OECD.Stat* (database), https://stats.oecd.org/Index.aspx?DataSetCode=LMPEXP.

However, the extent by which countries in Latin America allocate resources to training is rather heterogeneous. With the exception of Colombia and Chile, public spending for training measures in LAC countries is well below the OECD average. For instance, in Argentina, spending on training is roughly half that of the OECD average, and in Mexico and Brazil, funding allocated to training is almost non-existent (Figure 4.1). In Chile and Colombia, most expenditure on ALMPs are channelled into job-training courses and executed by the national training institutions (SENCE and SENA respectively), without a clear and holistic vision (OECD, 2018[1]; OECD, 2019[2]).

While the region has had a positive experience with a limited set of ALMPs, especially targeting younger workers (Box 4.1), policies to help adult workers transition from job to job are mainly absent and several commentators argue that those should be implemented (Busso et al., 2017[3]). Expanding the offer of training opportunities, which should also aim at including adults currently outside of the labour market, may therefore require spending more public resources on adult training.

> ### Box 4.1. Peru: The role of workfare programmes in boosting employment prospects and job quality
>
> #### From Construyendo Perú to Trabaja Perú
>
> The programme *Construyendo Perú,* was introduced in 2007 as a workfare programme, to address employability issues and provide income support to unemployed individuals mainly heads of households, in situations of poverty and extreme poverty. The new programme aimed to: (i) provide individuals with access to temporary employment; and (ii) help them enhance their employability, thus improving their chances of reintegration into the labour market. To achieve this, the programme provided short-term jobs and skills development through the financing of public investment projects that required intensive use of unskilled labour. The programme had therefore two components. The first was the creation of temporary jobs in public investment projects (e.g. pedestrian accesses, irrigation canals, post-harvest infrastructure, retaining walls and educational and health infrastructure). The second component entailed providing two types of training to participants in parallel with the public investment projects. The more general type of training provided a range of soft skills development, including social skills, empowerment and a general knowledge of how to oversee the implementation of projects. The second training element aimed to develop technical skills that would be appropriate to the needs of the labour market in the region – rather than to the project in question. Although the general training was mandatory, in practice it was not enforced. The more tailored training was voluntary, with take-up disproportionately high among individuals with higher levels of educational attainment.
>
> The training component was officially active from 2007 to 2010, and during this period the programme provided soft-skills training to close to 260 000 individuals and more tailored technical training to 27 000 (Macroconsult S.A., 2012[7]). Importantly, monitoring of the programme carried out by the Ministry of Economy and Finance (MEF) (Jaramillo, Baanante and Sanz, 2009[8]) revealed that by 2009 specific training had ceased to be provided by the programme. In practice, the specific training component was provided almost exclusively during 2007 and 2008, and even then it did not take place systematically. The training components suffered from additional implementation problems, which may have been the motivation for their cessation. For example, the MEF study points to important differences in the content and quality of the training provided in different districts. Moreover, the differences in duration of the short-term jobs created, meant that a number of individuals received training for a very short period of time.

> In 2011, a new programme, *Trabaja Perú*, was created and replaced *Construyendo Perú*. Like its predecessor, *Trabaja Perú* co-finances public investment projects that aim to create temporary jobs for the unemployed and underemployed whose incomes fall within poverty or extreme poverty levels in both urban and rural areas. The aim of the programme, in addition to creating short-term jobs, is to develop productive capacities for the most vulnerable, thereby promoting sustained and quality jobs for this segment of the population. It therefore replaces all of the functions of Construyendo Perú, with the exception of the training components, which were removed from the objectives of the programme in 2012.
>
> Source: ILO (2016[5]), *What Works: Active Labour Market Policies in Latin America and the Caribbean*, https://www.ilo.org/wcmsp5/groups/public/---dgreports/---dcomm/---publ/documents/publication/wcms_492373.pdf.

National Training Institutes are important players in Latin America adult learning systems, but their effectiveness should be improved

One way to support training in Latin America is to subsidise its supply through the creation of National Training Institutes (NTIs). NTIs are public agencies tasked to provide and oversee the supply of government-funded training. SENAI in Brazil or SENCE in Chile (see Box 4.2 on the programmes promoted in Chile by SENCE) along with SENA in Colombia, INA in Costa Rica, INADEH in Panama, and SNPP in Paraguay are examples of NTIs funded by a specific payroll tax. In the case of Colombia and Mexico funding comes from general resources, and in Chile most training occurs through private providers that receive government subsidies.

These institutes were originally created in the mid-20th century to train active workers in technical skills in the framework of the import-substitution industrialisation model. At that time, training the unemployed, job seekers with low levels of formal education, or other vulnerable groups such as women was not a central objective of the institutes. The government was responsible for the regulation and provision of training, and the content of the courses was determined centrally (supply-driven contents). In the 1980s and 1990s these institutes and training models came into scrutiny and then reformed to better respond to the needs of the labour market and to include under their umbrella other segments of the population such as the unemployed and the youth in their target population (Ibarrarán and Rosas-Shady, 2009[9]).

The reforms led to different organisational changes across countries. Some NTIs, for instance in Chile, Paraguay, Uruguay, El Salvador, have been converted into training administrators – no longer providing training directly – but issuing tenders to public or private training providers to offer courses that meet the specific demand of the labour market. In many other countries, such as Colombia, Ecuador, Honduras, Dominican Republic, Mexico and Panama, instead, NTIs still operate as training providers (Alaimo et al., 2015[10]; Ibarrarán and Rosas-Shady, 2009[9]).

The amount of resources channelled to NTIs varies among countries (Table 4.1). NTIs are financed with a specific tax on the payroll of formal workers that ranges from 0.25% (Uruguay) to 2% (Colombia) and even when these investments are sizable, the effectiveness of their action could be strengthened (Busso et al., 2017[3]). Several challenges hamper the effectiveness of NTIs.

First, training is provided only to a small fraction of employed workers. Evidence points that, in the region, less than 15% of employed workers have access to training from NTIs – the only exception is Colombia where up to 24% of workers are involved in training supplied by NTIs (Busso et al., 2017[3]). Evidence based on a representative survey of formal firms in five countries, namely the Bahamas, Colombia, Honduras, Panama and Uruguay, shows that, on average, less than 12% of firms makes use of public resources to finance their training initiatives, and when used, these funding generally go to large firms (González-Velosa C., Rosas D. and Flores R., 2016[11]).[2]

The weak take up of public resources to promote on-the-job training is likely to reflect the insufficient coverage of NTIs programmes but also the low quality and the lack of relevance of the training provided (Crespi, Fernández-Arias and Stein, 2014[12]). This calls for the need to reinforce the mechanisms to ensure that training is targeted to the sectors and occupations more in demand in the productive sector.

Second, the monitoring of the quality of the training could be strengthened. Mechanisms to measure the results and the impact of programmes are generally lacking along with independent bodies in charge of quality assurance of the courses. This situation can create an environment of little or no accountability, leading to training that in some cases is of low quality or that may not be fully adequate to the needs of employees and employers alike (Crespi, Fernández-Arias and Stein, 2014[12]).

Table 4.1. Characteristics of NTIs

	Institute	Contribution (% of payroll)	Contribution (% of GDP)	Training system
Chile	SENCE	n/a	0.100	1
Colombia	SENA	2.0	0.367	4
Dominican Republic	Infotep	1.0	0.070	4
Ecuador	Secap	0.5	0.030	2
El Salvador	Insaforp	1.0	0.120	4
Honduras	Infop	1.0	0.190	1
Panama	Inadeh*	1.5	0.290	2
Paraguay	Sinafocal	1.0	0.000	4
Uruguay	Inefop	0.25	0.043	1

Note: Type of training systems: 1 = administrator, 2 = almost always administrator, 3 = frequently provides training, 4 = always provides training.
*Inadeh was created by the Decree Law of 8 February 2006 and absorbed the former National Institute for Professional Training (Inaforp) and other training programmes, actions, resources, and initiatives under way. n/a = not applicable. In the case of Chile, it is not a payroll tax but an exemption of up to 1% of the tax on profits, based on the resources invested in training.
Source: Hunneus, C., C. de Mendoza and G. Rucci (2011[13]), "El estado del arte de la capacitación de los trabajadores en América Latina and el Caribe", *Technical Note*, No. 346.

Box 4.2. Examples of challenges in the training programmes offered by SENCE in Chile

In Chile, SENCE is the national training and employment service institution that depends on the Ministry of Labour and is responsible for adult learning. SENCE concentrates the largest number of beneficiaries for training programmes, 77% of the total in 2016. The system is articulated around: i) tax credits for on-the-job training (*Impulsa Personas* - ex. *Franquicia Tributaria*), ii) training programmes targeted primarily at vulnerable groups (e.g. *Más Capaz*) and iii) employment subsidies. Recent evidence highlights how the system is fragmented, leading to a diversity of programmes with similar purposes and target populations, including within the same agency. Agencies lack a mechanism to co-ordinate with each other resulting in dispersion of unconnected efforts among different public agencies lacking coherence.

Impulsa Persona (ex-Franquicia Tributaria) is the main training programme administered by SENCE. In 2016, this programme reached approximately 8% of the labour force. Tax credits to firms who send their workers on training with certified institutions are equivalent to around 30% of SENCE public spending on training in 2016 (OECD, 2018[14]).

> Several aspects of the programme could be strengthened. *Impulsa Persona*, for instance, benefits mostly large firms, which tend to employ more resilient, highly educated workers (Larrañaga et al., 2011[15]; Rodriguez and Urzúa, 2011[16]). The programmes also does not reach the self-employed, which have accounted for a large share of job creation in the latest years. Evaluation of the tax credit done by the National Productivity Commission has found the programme to be ineffective due to the short duration and lack of relevance of training programmes. The programme also lacks the requirement of certification of courses, and problems in the design of incentives for firms and the structure of suppliers and intermediaries, among others (Comisión Nacional de Productividad, 2018[17]; Bravo, García and Schlechter, 2019[18]). Most training programmes are fundamentally theoretical programmes; taught in classrooms, not in workshops or workplaces, and tend to measure their success by attendance and teaching hours rather than the gains in employability. Most do not include practical training or on-the-job training, and the skills acquired are not certified.
>
> *Màs capaz* is the flagship programme for skills and employability development targeting the most vulnerable: youth, low-skilled workers and women. It represents another 30% of public spending allocated to SENCE in 2016. The programme provide short-term training, labour intermediation services and certification of competencies. In 2016, the programme reached around 5% of the target population. Evidence suggests that the programme works better for the unemployed than for the inactive (Brown et al., 2016[19]).
>
> Source: OECD (2018[14]), *OECD Economic Surveys: Chile 2018*, https://dx.doi.org/10.1787/eco_surveys-chl-2018-en; Larrañaga, O. et al (2011[15]), *Informe Final. Comisión Revisora Del Sistema de Capacitación e Intermediación Laboral*, https://www.undp.org/content/dam/chile/docs/pobreza/undp_cl_pobreza_InformeFinal_211011_doc2.pdf; Rodriguez, J. and S. Urzúa (2011[16]), *An Evaluation of Training Programs Financed by Public Funds in Chile*; Comisión Nacional de Productividad (2018[17]), "Formación de Competencias para el Trabajo en Chile", https://www.comisiondeproductividad.cl/estudios/formacion-de-competencias-para-el-trabajo-en-chile/; Bravo, J., A. García and H. Schlechter (2019[18]), "Mercado Laboral Chileno para la Cuarta Revolución Industrial - Clapes UC", *Documentos de Trabajo*, No. 59, http://www.clapesuc.cl/investigaciones/doc-trabajo-no59-mercado-laboral-chileno-para-la-cuarta-revolucion-industrial/. Brown, C. et al. (2016[19]), *Primer año del Programa + Capaz. Evidencia sobre Inserción laboral de Egresados*.

Initiatives to align skill supply to the demand of Latin America in the era of digitalisation and automation

In a context of rapidly changing skill demands in the labour market, it is crucial to equip workers with the ICT skills needed for the digital transformation. While digitalisation has been slow in making its way in Latin America [see Chapter 1 and (OECD/IDB, 2016[20])], new digital technologies are certainly going to reshape future labour market and societal demands. LAC governments are also already making important steps towards the design of training interventions aimed at responding to the skill challenges that more connected and digital labour markets will soon bring about. Several programmes to enhance general and specialised ICT skills have been deployed in the region.

In Mexico, for instance, 32 Digital Inclusion Centres (Puntos Mexico Conectado – Centros de Inclusión Digital) were set up across the country, providing basic digital skills programmes. The aim of the initiative is to bridge the digital divide and enhance broadband internet access for all. Centres are operating in each state of Mexico and the initiative targeted to marginalised areas with high poverty rates. In terms of the content, the "*Puntos México Conectado*" programme aims to provide digital literacy, programing, coding, innovation and entrepreneurship courses free of charge to enable a greater digital inclusion and generate better-informed and more community-involved citizens. Similarly, the programme wants to promote the creation of more efficient and productive micro, small and medium enterprises throughout the country. In addition, the programme has also been used to bridge gender gaps and encourage young girls to approach ICT skill development. As of now, 54% of the enrolled students are young girls.

In 2012, Peru passed the National Digital Literacy Plan. This plans aims to train individuals in ICT skills, the use of computer tools as well as mobile devices. Around 107 online courses were made available also to teachers as part of the *Educate Peru Programme* with emphasis also on developing digital skills to incorporate ICT use in the classroom. At the end of the programme, over 25 000 teachers had received training on line and approximately 2 000 taking courses on integrating ICTs in the classroom. In addition, the Peruvian PRONABEC (the public agency in charge of granting scholarships) provides grants to graduate and college students to engage in ICT-related careers in national universities and abroad and the national Council for Science and Technology (CONCYTEC) finances postgraduate studies and research in ICT.

In similar ways, both Costa Rica and Brazil have been devoting resources to finance the development of ICT skills. Costa Rica's state universities, for instance, offer ICT training courses for the general population, particularly its vulnerable segments (e.g. the elderly and disabled).[3] In Brazil, the programme Science without Borders sponsors graduate studies and research abroad for Brazilians supporting, also, foreign researchers to carry out research in Brazil's priority development areas.

As digital technologies spread across the region, online learning offers a significant opportunity to leverage broadband network access to spread knowledge across the economy in a cost-effective way.

Online learning can take many forms. It can be delivered as traditional university-style courses online, or as informal training related to specific work skills or lifetime learning activities. One advantage of online learning relative to traditional learning is that this provides opportunities for individuals in remote areas to access relevant material, irrespective of their location and, potentially, at a cheaper cost.

Massive Open Online Courses (MOOCs), academic courses offered online often provided at no cost, aim at large-scale interactive participation from around the world. From an operational point of view, MOOCs avoid the cost of setting up expensive training boot camps whose effects are limited in time. Second, their flexible structure allows learners to go through the materials at their own pace, while motivating them to collaborate on common learning objectives.

However, despite the tremendous possibilities offered by the use of digital technologies for learning, challenges emerge. In the context of LAC countries, in particular, the potential availability of technical solutions to connect students to learning opportunities face the challenge that not all students will be ICT-proficient and able to access these training opportunities. According to Survey of Adult Skills (PIAAC) data, in fact, individuals who are more likely to participate in open education in Latin America, as across OECD countries more broadly are mainly young, educated and skilled workers (Figure 4.2). Evidence also suggests that open courses are mostly used by those who combine work and formal education and to a lesser extent by those who are only employed. Much needs to be done by policy makers and training providers to make online training truly available to the low skilled.

Second, MOOCS and online courses do not usually lead to a certification, a qualification or a title that can be used in the labour market to signal one's credentials and skills. Across many OECD countries (and more so in Latin America where online courses are still in their infancy), micro-credentials are mostly unregulated and the validation of contents and of quality varies very much across the spectrum of available training options. This poses several challenges to the use of MOOCs and online courses as the lack of a certification framework hinders their acceptance.

Figure 4.2. Open education in Latin America

% of each category

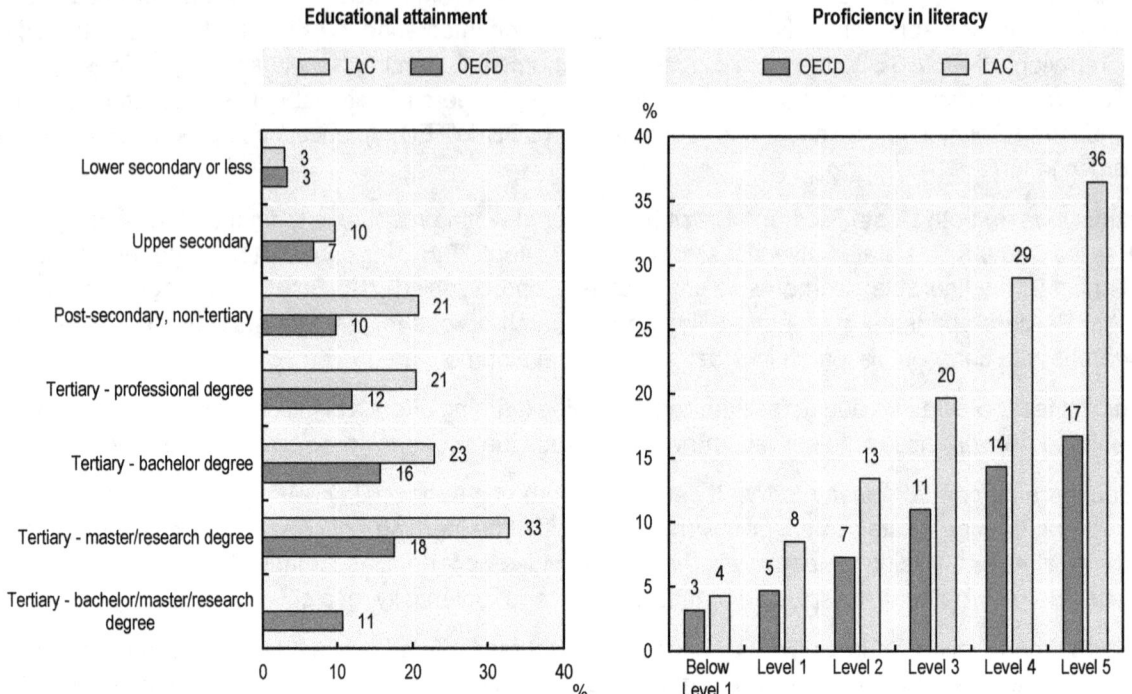

Source: OECD calculations based on OECD (2017[21]), Survey of Adults Skills (PIAAC) (2012, 2015, 2017) (database), http://www.oecd.org/skills/piaac/.

Tools and initiatives to assess and respond to future skill needs

Information about the quality of adult learning programmes in Latin America is rather scarce. Some evidence, however, seems to point out that Latin America, education and training systems may not be oriented to economic development (Alaimo et al., 2015[10]) and that strengthening the alignment of training content to employers' needs would be required.

There are several ways to ensure this alignment. In first instance, the content of adult learning programmes has to be responsive to current (and future) skills needs in the labour market. For this, governments need to build data collection infrastructures to timely analyse their labour market and systems and for this information to feed into curricula revision.

The most common approaches used by governments and ministries include the development of medium-term occupational forecasts or of assessments of current skill needs that draw from labour market information (usually labour force surveys) or vacancy surveys.

Several challenges lie ahead of the policy maker when trying to develop effective tools to assess, anticipate and respond to skill demands. One major risk, for instance, is that the Skill Assessment and Anticipation (SAA) exercise may not be well aligned with the potential policy uses. For instance, the way skills are defined has to be useful for policy making, providing an output that the policy maker can understand and whose results are sufficiently disaggregated at the regional, sub-regional or sectoral levels for the policy makers to be able to use them.

However, skills are difficult to measure and there may be no strict correspondence between how skills are understood in the skills development process (e.g. formal education credentials) and what is required in the labour market (e.g. specific occupations). Skill needs are commonly approximated by measuring which occupations are, or will be, in greater or lesser demand as they mirror economic projections. Given the need for planning in the education system, skills are also frequently approximated by qualifications (e.g. technical/vocational, university), fields of study (e.g. law, medicine, economics, catering) or, to a lesser extent, by measuring specific cognitive or non-cognitive skills (e.g. numeracy, literacy, soft skills, etc.) (OECD, 2016[22]).

Bearing these challenges in mind, some countries in Latin America have implemented good initiatives to improve labour market information.

In Chile, for instance, the Public Employment Service (PES) uses information on labour demand, collected through interviews, surveys and roundtables, to align their training offer with labour market needs. In addition, the government runs an online portal called the National Employment Exchange (BNE), (www.bne.cl.) a free site where companies publish job offers and workers can submit CVs for consideration. In addition to offering job matching, the BNE portal also contains links to programmes, training and career guidance. Mexico has several programmes to link students, teachers and jobs. The "*Circuito conectados contigo*" portal ("Circuit connected to you") helps companies match with both students and teachers.[4] In 2013, the "Total Uni" portal was launched to help high school students to connect to jobs in the labour market (Total Uni) (www.totaluni.com).

In the Dominican Republic, the Ministry of Labour created a job portal that matches employers with potential workers. Candidates can register their information and apply to jobs. In September 2015, 11 000 businesses were listed on the platform and nearly 42 000 jobs posted.[5]

In Brazil, as part of the *Pronatec* programme, different ministries can submit requests to the Ministry of Education for creating specific training programmes that correspond to the identified needs. The Ministry of Education centralises these requests and coordinates the opening of funded training programmes with public and private training providers. The training opportunities under the *Pronatec* programme are therefore, in principle, restricted to areas of identified needs. However, OECD (2018[1]) finds that in practice the training offered under *Pronatec* generally does not correspond to skill needs, but mainly reflects the capacities and preferences of training providers. In addition, Brazil has a publicly certified platform for CVs managed by the National Centre of Scientific Research, the CNPQ (*Lattes platform*) (http://lattes.cnpq.br/). It is often used by university graduates. In September 2015, the site hosted nearly 1.2 million CVs.

Although some countries in the region have made good efforts in setting up information systems, job market information can be made more accessible and used more effectively in combination with career guidance and mentoring to support students (and adults more generally) in their training decisions.

Private-sector supported training in Latin America

Information on employers' engagement in adult learning provision is limited, especially when it comes to internationally comparable data. While previous studies shows that on-the-job training positively impact both workers' wages and firms' productivity and innovation (Almeida, Behrman and Robalino, 2012[23]), in Latin America, as in most other countries, too many employers are hesitant to provide on-the-job training.

Several challenges lie ahead and market failures make employers and employees to invest sub-optimally in job-specific training (OECD, 2017[24]). Available evidence[6] suggests that firms very rarely supply training in transferable skills in particular. Employers are in many cases reluctant to provide such training, fearing that workers could leave the firm in search of a premium for their newly acquired skills somewhere else. Conversely, employers have greater incentives to provide job-specific skills training that are immediately useful in production.

According to Flores Lima, González-Velosa and Rosas-Shady (2014[25]), and based on the World Bank Enterprise Survey, between 30% to 50% of LAC firms in the manufacturing sector offered their workers training through short, structured courses focusing on specific job-related skills. This is a relatively large share of firms, especially when compared to other developing countries in different areas of the world. However, the average figures mask great heterogeneity across firms of different sizes, with SMEs participating in training activities much less than larger firms in the region.

Large variation in the number of people involved in training is also recorded across countries (Figure 4.3). Evidence shows that firms in Latin America train between 49% (in Chile) and 78% (in Ecuador) of their workers, though no information is available about the duration of the training nor on training provided by firms in the informal sector, which represent the vast majority of firms in LAC countries.[7]

In addition, the highly skilled workers are more likely to benefit from these courses and get more out of them: the share of workers that receives training is higher for skilled than for low skilled workers (Flores Lima, González-Velosa and Rosas-Shady, 2014[25]).

Figure 4.3. Incidence and intensity of on-the-job training in formal firms in Latin America

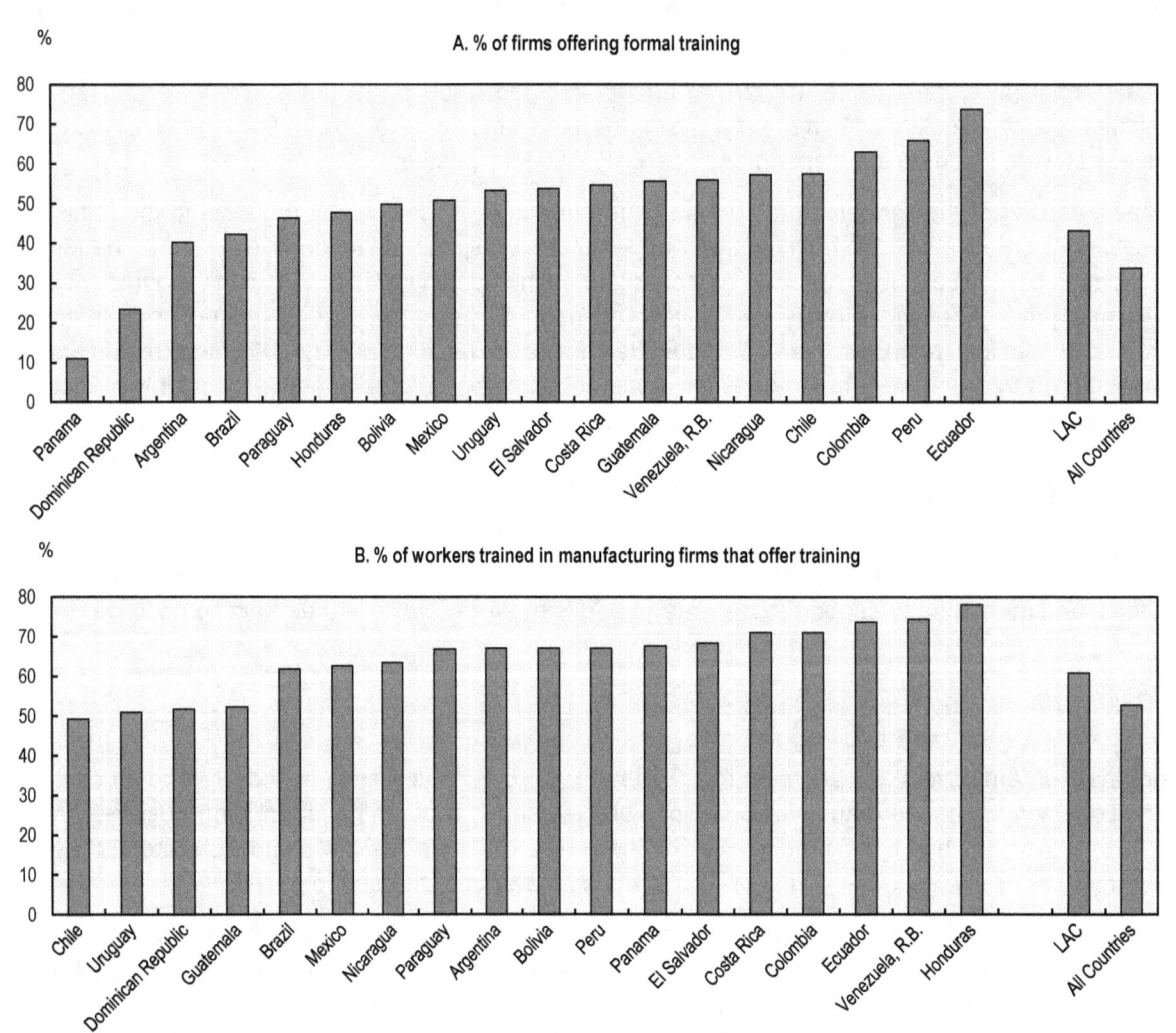

Note: Data refer to 2017 for Argentina, the Plurinational State of Bolivia, Colombia, Ecuador, Guatemala, Peru and Uruguay; to 2016 for El Salvador, the Dominican Republic and Honduras; to 2010 for the Bolivarian Republic of Venezuela, Chile, Costa Rica, Mexico and Panama and to 2009 for Brazil.
Source: Adapted from the World Bank. (2009[26]), *World Bank Enterprise Survey, 2009-2017*, https://microdata.worldbank.org/index.php/catalog/enterprise_surveys.

Results from the OECD Survey of Adults Skills (PIAAC) offer some additional insights to assess the involvement of firms in workers' training. On average across LAC countries participating in the survey, 63% of workers report to have received funding from their employers for at least one learning activities. Mexico has the largest share of workers participating in training activities in the region, with about 80% participating in training. Ecuador has the lowest share (around 60%) pointing to the fact that while many firms in Ecuador engage in training (more than 73%), training covers only part of their employees and that inclusiveness could be strengthened.

Figure 4.4. Employers' investment in training could be improved

% of participants who have received funding from their employer for at least one learning activity

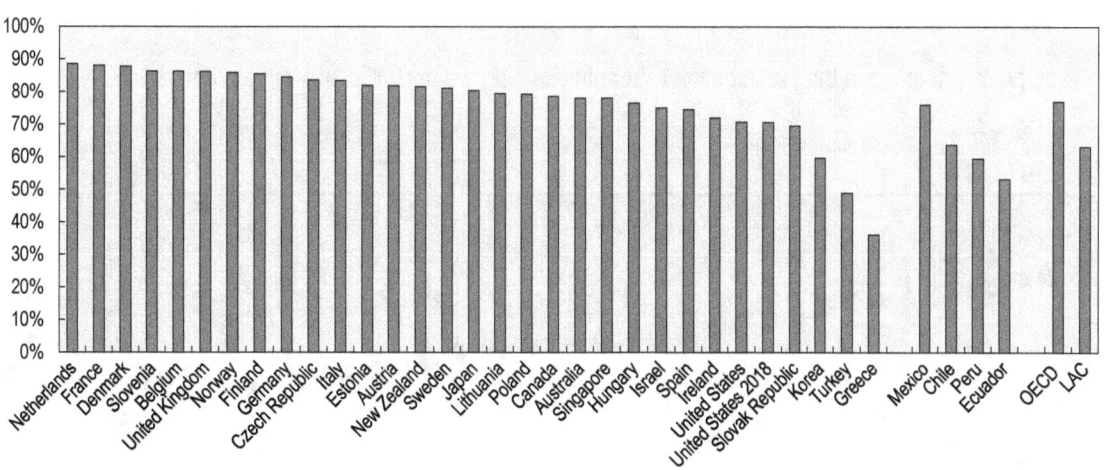

Note: Data on employer spending refer to formal or non-formal job-related adult learning.
Source: OECD (2019[27]), Priorities for Adult Learning dashboard, http://www.oecd.org/employment/skills-and-work/adult-learning/dashboard.htm.

The size and managerial quality of LAC firms help to explain participation in training

SMEs are less likely to provide training to their workers

In Latin America, smaller firms are less likely to provide training to workers than larger firms. Data from PIAAC show that only 40% of workers in SMEs participated in training, compared to 69% workers in larger firms. While a similar pattern can be found in all other countries participating in the Survey of Adult Skills (PIAAC), in Latin America the gap in training provision between small and large firms is almost twice as large (approx. 30%) as the OECD average (17%).

This gap, that in Mexico and Ecuador is even greater than 30%, is particularly worrying and represents a key challenge for Latin America, considering that SMEs account for more than 80% of employment and more than 90% of firms in the region.[8] By engaging less in training, SMEs are potentially missing great opportunities for growth and development.

Management quality is generally low in the region

Evidence for Latin America shows that the positive relationship between training and firms is likely to hold especially when firms have developed adequate managerial skills to allow returns from investment in human capital to materialise in productivity gains. At the firm level, high skill use is associated with higher productivity. What happens inside the workplace – the way work is organised and jobs are designed as well as the management practices adopted by the firm – is a key determinant of how skills are used (OECD, 2019[28]). In particular, it has been argued that better skill use and managerial skills are important in explaining the differences in productivity among firms and countries and go hand in hand with firms' productivity, workers' engagement and innovation (Bloom and Van Reenen, 2007[29]). Measure of management practices in large firms in the manufacturing sector are estimated to explain between 20% to 50% of the total factor productivity (TFP) gap between different countries.

Evidence from Flores Lima, González-Velosa and Rosas-Shady (2014[25]) shows that an increase in the proportion of skilled workers increases the productivity of manufacturing firms with more than 100 employees. In particular, it is estimated that a 1% increase in the share of high-skilled workers could lead, on average, up to a 0.7% increase in productivity in large firms.

Figure 4.5. SMEs are less likely to provide training to their workers

Percentage point difference in the participation rate between workers in SMEs and large enterprises

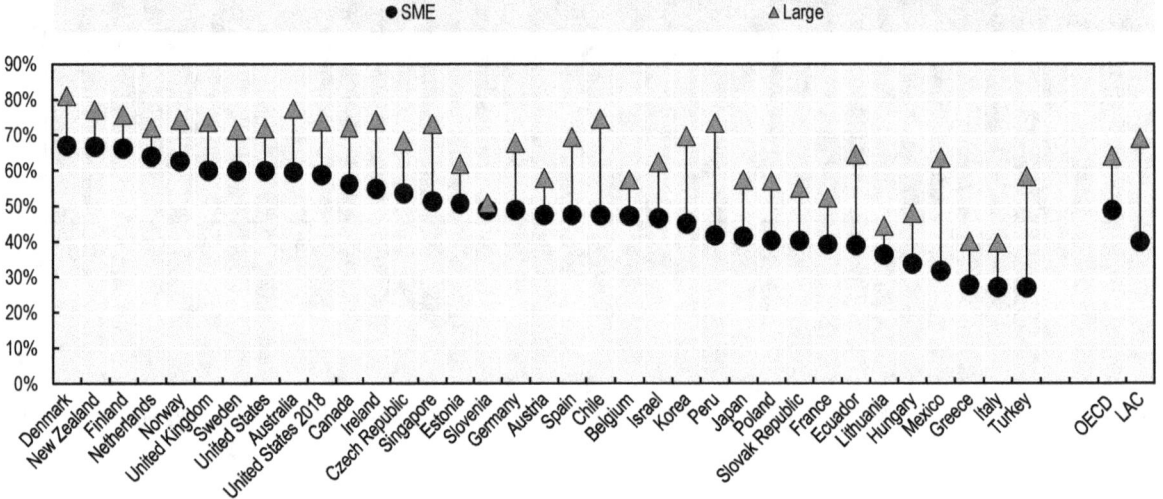

Source: OECD (2019[27]), Priorities for Adult Learning dashboard, http://www.oecd.org/employment/skills-and-work/adult-learning/dashboard.htm.

Managerial skills are, however, relatively low in many LAC firms. Evidence from the World Management Survey (Figure 4.6) shows that managerial quality in LAC countries stands below that of the OECD average and that firms are more poorly run than across OECD countries. The performance is especially low in countries such as Colombia or Brazil, while firms in Mexico reach OECD-average standards. This suggests that few managers in the region follow the best management practices and many would benefit from receiving training in this area. Interventions aiming at adopting more effective managerial practices in the region could lead firms to better utilise existing skills and reap the productivity gains, increasing returns to training for all.

Figure 4.6. Management score, average 2004-2015

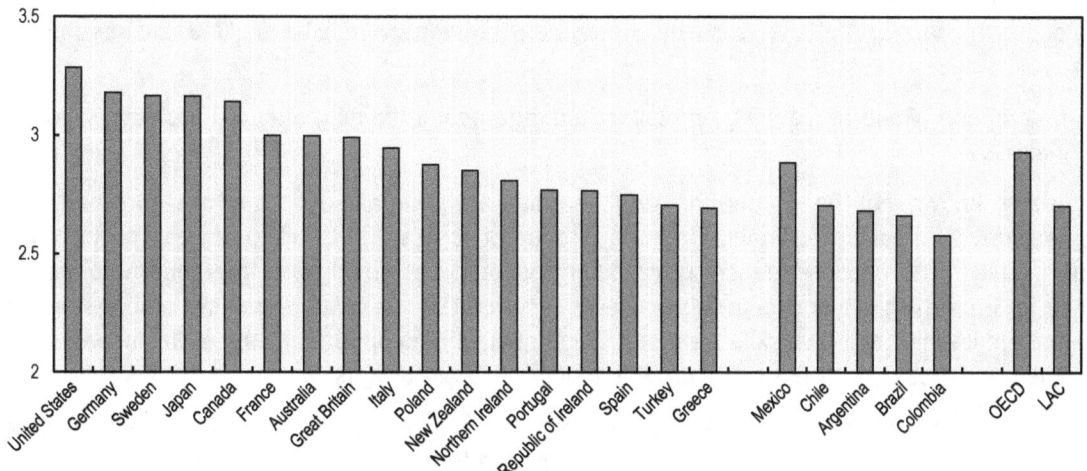

Source: Adapted from the World Management Survey (2015[30]), World Management Survey 2015, https://worldmanagementsurvey.org.

A coherent approach is needed: The role of a whole-of-stakeholders approach

Boosting the participation of individuals and firms in adult learning calls for a holistic approach and for the recognition that the different actors that are involved in adult learning may respond differently to specific sets of incentives. Failure to engage each actor of the system with targeted interventions can hinder the overall participation and promote an unequal participation in adult learning (OECD, 2019[31]).

Barriers to the participation of *individuals* in adult learning, for instance, usually relate to their lack of motivation, financial and time constraints or limited awareness of the potential benefits of participating in training. Those barriers, however, can affect different groups of individuals in different ways. High-skilled workers, for instance, may be more prone to engage in training than low-skilled workers are as they are usually better informed about the potential benefits of life-long learning and face fewer financial constraints. Low skilled workers, on the other hand, may face stronger barriers to participate in adult learning as they lack adequate ICT skills or face more pressing time constraints.

Similarly, the incentives needed to boost the participation of *firms* in adult learning may differ from those required to engage individuals. While some firms, for instance, may see training as a means to fill *narrow* skill gaps that are hindering productivity growth, individuals might prefer to engage in training that ensures the development of portable and more *transversal* skills. Likewise, the training needs of workers employed in firms of different sizes may also be very different and, as such, the strategies pursued by firms to fill those gaps and the incentives needed to engage them effectively in adult learning.

Making sense of the variety of different actors and of the differences in the motivations to participate in adult learning represent an important challenge for the policy-maker who needs to strike the necessary balance between different sets of incentives while boosting participation for all.

How to balance public and private investment and involve employers in supplying training activities

As mentioned above, there are many reasons why employers should invest in developing the skills of their workforce. By keeping employees' skills up to date, for instance, firms can adopt or introduce new technologies in their workflow and remain competitive, increasing productivity and profits.

However, a range of market failures and barriers such as the lack of information, capacity and/or resources mean that the amount of investments in education and training by employers could be sub-optimal, particularly in the case of SMEs. This is why government intervention may be justified and needed (OECD, 2017[24]).

Policy intervention aimed at fostering employers' engagement in training may require acting along three different axes.

First, it is well known that the returns from adult learning are generally difficult to measure and, as such, employers may be hesitant to finance training directly or to grant time off to workers to participate in learning activities. As a consequence, governments should be providing more robust information and guidance to firms as this is crucial to raise awareness about the benefits of training amongst employers and help them identify their own skills needs and potential funding opportunities (i.e. tax incentives, levies or subsidies) that could be leveraged to provide training to their workers.

Second, given that much of adult learning takes place at work and in the firm, policy intervention should be aimed at building the capacity of employers to provide truly relevant training to their workers and to understand and plan on what skills will be needed in the future. Employers, especially those operating in small firms, lack the resources to carry out sophisticated workforce planning exercises and to provide training accordingly. Governments, therefore, can act in both cases by supporting and targeting specific firms with subsidies to build skills development capacity and reduce training costs while also strengthening their efficacy.

Third, and more generally, policy makers may consider setting up well-designed financial incentives to boost engagement in training, trying to strike the right balance between the support to firms and individuals, on the one hand, and the prevention of potential deadweight losses, on the other. These three aspects are analysed more in detail below.

Providing information and guidance to employers is crucial, especially in the case of small and medium enterprises

Often times, employers are not aware of the importance of training nor have a clear understanding of how to develop the skills of their workforce to benefit from technological change and innovation. As a consequence, many employers may be reluctant to invest in training as they might not be able to clearly identify the positive returns to such investments and fear the possibility that other employers would poach their most skilled employees.

Providing concrete evidence of the benefits stemming from job-related learning activities on productivity and employee retention and workers engagement can act as a powerful incentive for employers to engage in training (OECD/ILO, 2017[32]).

In this context, government intervention can help a great deal by setting up tailored guidance, information campaigns and other initiatives focused on raising awareness of the benefits of training investment and better skills use, disseminating good practice and sharing expert advice are key.

This support is especially important for SMEs which, in many instances, lack the capacity to assess their skills beyond the very short-term and to plan relevant training activities to help the development of their business (Ellis, 2003[33]).

Two intertwined challenges emerge. On the one hand, as mentioned, managerial quality is relatively low in LAC countries and especially in SMEs. On the other hand, SMEs lack sufficient resources to address skill challenges individually. Providing targeted coaching to employers to help them develop managerial skills to identify their own firm's skill needs and develop an appropriate training offer is crucial.

Creating employer networks can be a solution to both challenges as these often provide leadership and management skills programmes, in addition to their role as facilitators of knowledge exchange and capacity building. Networks of employers have, in fact, the advantage of pooling the resources of smaller actors together, creating a critical mass and economies of scale that SMEs can leverage to their own advantage (and that would have been impossible to create if small employers had to act individually).

Skillnet Ireland, for instance, is an example of enterprises joining forces to deliver adult learning. It is based on the premise that groups of employers in the same sector or region would have similar training needs and, therefore, that they would be interested in sharing the cost of training delivery. *Skillnet*, funded through training levies, currently consists of 66 learning networks, which include over 15 000 companies, most of which (94%) are SMEs in the agricultural or services sector. In 2017, over EUR 30.2 million were invested in 6 000 upskilling and training programmes for almost 50 000 people (OECD, 2019[34]).

In Australia, the Industry Reference Committees (IRCs) also play an important role in assessing and anticipating changing skill needs of different economic sectors. Each year the IRCs develop an "*industry skills forecast*" (ISF)[9] to identify skills gaps, emerging skill needs and associated training needs for the whole industry sector, leading to an assessment of whether there is a need to update training packages (OECD, 2018[35]). In doing so, IRCs consult widely with key industry stakeholders to develop the ISFs and disseminate precious information to all firms in the sector.

In other countries, government-supported management training programmes are available to employers, often with a focus on SMEs. A good example is the United Kingdom, where eight innovative projects to develop leadership and entrepreneurship skills in SMEs received government support as part of the UK Futures Programme (OECD, 2019[28]).

Similarly, the French Occupation and Skills Observatories (*Observatoires Prospectifs des Métiers et des Qualifications*: OPMQ), jointly funded by employers' organisations and trade unions, carries out skill planning activities benefitting all firms in the economy. These activities encompass the mapping or listing occupations in high demand, as well as surveys and analyses on skills management, training and recruitment needs, and the creation of certification schemes.

The government, through its subsidiaries and agencies can also support directly firms in developing a response to skill challenges. An interesting example of this type of initiatives is the Joint Purchase Training *(Yhteishankinoulutus)* in Finland. This programme, offered by the PES, aims at supporting employers who want to retrain existing staff or set-up training activities for new recruits. The programme helps employers identify the training needs, select the appropriate candidates for training and help them participate in the procurement and planning of that training (i.e. find an education provider who can deliver the tailored training). This programme also helps building a positive learning culture in the company that can further foster training participation.

Similarly, in Flanders (Belgium), the government-funded Centres for Adult Basic Education send "ambassadors" to companies to review work-based learning opportunities and discuss the benefits of providing these opportunities within the company. They then aim to find ways to give more room to work-based learning, in particular for the low skilled (OECD, 2019[28]).

In many countries, social partners are also heavily involved in the adult learning system and they play a key role in building the capacity of employers to train for the future. In Germany, for instance, the initiative Securing the Skilled Labour Base: Vocational Training and Education (CVET) (Fachkräfte sichern: weiterbilden und Gleichstellung fördern) supports employers in increasing adult learning participation and gender equality at work. Funding is provided for five types of activities: i) creation of staff development structures (i.e. training centres), particularly for skill upgrading; ii) creation of interlinked CVET structures for SMEs; iii) initiate dialogue across branches of industry; iv) strengthen the ability of business stakeholders to promote equality of opportunity; and v) develop work time models and career pathways adapted to phases in a worker's life. Companies receive coaching and training to analyse their staff's skills and training needs and they learn practical ways of implementing/creating staff development structures and on how to work with partners (OECD, 2019[31]).

Effective financial incentives to encourage employers participation in adult learning

There are several and important reasons for allowing the market (and not government intervention) to steer education and training decisions. When the correct incentives are in place, the choices of individuals and firms usually minimise costs and lead to greater benefits for society (OECD, 2017[24]). However, when certain pre-conditions are lacking, market failures can emerge and, as such, an inefficient allocation of resources and sub-optimal outcomes.

Among the risks associated to allowing training decisions to be determined solely by the market is that of insufficient participation in training as some groups of individuals may lack sufficient incentives to engage or firms may under-invest due to uncertainty, myopic behaviours or asymmetries of information.

In those cases, well-designed financial incentives aligned with government priorities can be useful tools to boost incentives to participate in training. There are important caveats however, when implementing financial incentives and benefits as well as drawbacks should be considered (Table 4.2). As with any policy intervention, a key challenge is to ensure the effectiveness of the incentives while minimising potential deadweight losses.

A few considerations are important. The design of financial incentives needs to consider the institutional context as well as the specific objectives that such policy intervention is meant to achieve. Before introducing any intervention, the policy maker should carefully assess the reasons for any apparent under-investment in training and the best way to create (or restore) adequate incentives. This means, in other words, that the policy intervention (the financial incentives) needs to be well targeted to address the specific challenge at hand. To complicate things, financial incentives come in different shapes and forms. These can be training or wage subsidies, tax incentives (direct tax cuts, tax credits) or levy schemes/training funds. Within this wide array of options, some types of financial incentives will be better suited to address the lack of motivation to participate in training while others, for instance, will be more efficient in spurring the development of transversal and portable skills in firms. The choice of the specific type of intervention is, therefore, crucial to achieve sound results with minimum deadweight loss and waste of public funding.

In addition, the efficacy of financial incentives depends on a range of framework conditions being in place in the country. For instance, while providing financial support to firms may be desirable to reduce the cost associated to participating in training, doing so without setting up a solid skills information system, helping employers make informed education decisions on the choice of education providers or on the skills to be developed may lead to considerable misuse of resources.

If the objective is to fill emerging technical skill gaps in the labour market, the government may consider promoting financial incentives that directly target employers. These can come in the shape of tax credits to invest in training or direct subsidies to promote learning in the firm.

Targeting financial incentives at employers rather than at individuals has the advantage that training is more likely to meet the specific needs of employers and, therefore, to fill gaps in labour market needs. One drawback, however, is that, by providing direct and unconditional support to employers through cash transfers, the government risks not being able to reach disadvantaged and vulnerable workers as employers have weaker incentives to provide training to those groups (OECD, 2017[24]).

Table 4.2. Benefits and drawbacks of training levies and tax incentives for firms

Financial incentive	Benefits	Drawbacks
Training Levies	Promote direct employers engagement and make them pro-active players of the adult learning system by giving them responsibility in training decisions. They bear a direct link with current labour market demands as this is an employer-driven strategy where firms are able to shape the training choices.	It requires firms to understand well their skill needs. This may be difficult to achieve for smaller firms that do not always have a good view of their own needs. These measure need to be accompanied by support and guidance to smaller firms. Larger firms are usually more likely to use these schemes and to benefit from it than SMEs. Identifying the adequate amount to be invested in the levy may be difficult in practice and this may lead to deadweight losses.
Tax-incentives for firms	Promote the pro-active engagement of firms that are benefiting from it by providing financial incentives firms to invest in training and to decide on what skills would be best for them to invest in. Incentives can be targeted to specific skill areas that are in need in the overall labour market and/or to disadvantaged groups of individuals. Tax incentives usually have a lower administration costs than other strategies as they leverage the pre-existing national infrastructure for tax collection.	Since the incentives are usually designed by the government, tax incentives are more effective when there exist a robust labour market intelligence system at the country level that can support the design of the policy intervention. Deadweight losses can emerge if tax incentives are not well targeted and if, for instance, they reach disproportionately those employers and firms that would have provided training anyways (usually larger and more competitive firms). It is important that the policy maker carefully target the incentive to firms with suboptimal levels of training or that face more pressing financial constraints (e.g. SMEs).

Solutions can be found so that the financial incentive is designed to reach employers under the condition that these provide training to most disadvantaged workers. The Training Grant for Employers in Estonia, for instance, covers between 50% and 100% of the training expenditures (with a cap) incurred by the employer. The exact amount of the incentive, however, depends on the age, educational level and employment history of the participant- where larger cash transfers are provided to those employers targeting disadvantaged individuals (OECD, 2019[28]).

Funds can also be made conditional on supplying training to the unemployed to ensure their re-inclusion in the labour market. An example among the numerous subsidies for employers to train the unemployed is the Individual Job Training (Individuele Beroepsopleiding – IBO) in Flanders (Belgium). This programme allows employers to hire a jobseeker and, with the help of the public employment service, to train her/him in the workplace over a period of one to six months, following a jointly established training plan.

Tax incentives (e.g. reductions/exemptions in social security contributions) are another alternative commonly used in both OECD and LAC economies to encourage employers' investments in training. In Chile, tax incentives are available to train workers even before they are hired (Impulsa Persona ex Franquia Tributaria: Pre contrato). These training activities can last for up to two months. The objective of the programme is to develop or improve the skills of future workers in order to increase their employability, but there is no obligation for the employer to hire the individual at the end of the training. Other examples of subsidies to train unemployed in LAC countries are the many *Jóvenes* Programmes (see Box 3.2) that are currently targeting vulnerable youth.

As part of Impulsa Personas, Chilean firms also receive a tax credit on the costs incurred in providing training or Recognition of Prior Learning (RPL) up to a maximum of 1% annual wages. Similarly, in Argentina, firms can receive tax credit when their workers participate in any type of learning (i.e. formal basic education, professional training, RPL, or on-the-job training). Due to the predominance of the NTIs as instruments to provide training, the take up of tax credit has been low in the region (Alaimo et al., 2015[10]).

Tax incentives and subsidies for SMEs have been used in different countries and some of those examples can inspire LAC countries

Tax incentives can be especially important tools to engage SMEs in training and, therefore, a suitable solution to overcome the weak participation in adult learning of smaller firms in many LAC countries. A number of different approaches can be used. In particular, tax incentives could be designed to help SMEs overcome cost barriers (e.g. Chèque Formation in Wallonia, Belgium; Profi!Lehre and Weiter!Bilden in Austria; Consortium for HRD Ability Magnified Program (CHAMP) in Korea). Other approaches, instead, specifically seek to help SMEs grow and become more competitive through skills investments (Industry Skills Fund in Australia, KMO Portefeuille in Flanders, Belgium) (OECD, 2017[24]).

The Formação-Ação in Portugal, for instance, focuses on a particular barrier to SME growth, namely management skills which is particularly important also across many SMEs in LAC countries. In particular, Formação-Ação combines classroom training, action in the company and individualised consultancy, with a view to developing the skills of managers and consequently increasing the competitiveness of SMEs. The programme covers specific thematic areas going from the implementation of management systems, the internationalisation of the firms and investment management. The Formação-Ação training activities are reimbursed up to 90% to companies, excluding the remuneration of teaching staff employed in supplying the training.

Subsidies and grants can also be used to target SMEs and help them engage in training. In Latvia, the training support for enhancing the competitiveness of enterprises covers 80% instead of 60% of the costs of general training and 45% instead of 35% of the costs of special training when the firm is an SME. While in Poland, the grants awarded through the National Training Fund cover 100% of the costs of lifelong learning for micro-enterprises, compared to 80% for all other firms.

Another set of programmes is open to firms of all sizes, but provides larger subsidies to SMEs. For example, the Crédit-Adaptation in Wallonia (Belgium) offers EUR 6-7 per training hour to large firms, and EUR 9-10 to SMEs. In France, employers with fewer than 250 employees receive an additional EUR 1 000 subsidy if they take on an apprentice.

In Finland, training offered as part of the Joint Purchase Training covers 30-50% of the costs, depending on the size of the company. The idea behind this programme is to support SMEs in building the capacity to identify their training needs and, eventually, to actually deliver the training. The Joint Purchase Training (Yhteishankintakoulutus), in fact, supports employers who want to retrain existing staff or set-up training programmes for newly recruited staff. Offered by the PES, it supports employers to define their training needs, select the appropriate candidates for training and find an education provider to deliver the tailored training. The PES also part-finances the training. There are different types of training that can be targeted to specific needs: i) Tailored Training (TäsmäKoulutus) for employers who want to retrain their staff due to technological or other changes in the sector (min. training duration 10 days); ii) Recruitment Training (RekryKoulutus) for employers who cannot find employees with the skills needed and want to hire, then train new staff (training duration 3-9 months); and iii) Change Training (MuutosKoulutus) for employers who have staff that has become redundant and help them transition to other job opportunities (training duration 10 days to 2 years).

In Japan, several programmes provide greater subsidies to SMEs, including: Career Keisei Sokushin Joseikin (which covers half the training costs of SMEs, compared to just a third for large firms); Career-up Josei-kin (which provides larger wage subsidies and higher ceilings on training costs for SMEs); and the Subsidy for Securing and Developing Skilled Construction Workers (which covers 90% of the cost of training for SMEs, compared to 50% for larger firms).

Another approach is to provide more flexibility and/or simpler procedures for SMEs. For example, in the Canada Job Fund Agreements, employers can apply for up to CAD 10 000 in government contributions toward the direct costs of training, such as tuition and training material – and they are required to contribute, on average, an additional 1/3 to these training costs. However, small businesses, with 50 or fewer employees, can benefit from more flexible funding arrangements, such as the possibility to count wages as half of their employer contribution or contribute a minimum of 15% (OECD, 2017[24]).

Training levies can be a good alternative to incentivise adult learning investment in Latin America

Levy systems are another option through which countries incentivise employers to contribute to the financing of adult learning (UNESCO, 2018[36]; OECD, 2019[28]). Training levies are a way to pool resources from employers and allocate them for expenditure on training. They are a form of collaborative solution, but differ from those that were discussed above in that, generally, they do not involve a government subsidy. Training levies can emerge either as a result of government political will (establishing the legislative framework for the levies to work) and/or from the initiative of social partners.

Levies ensure that employers contribute to adult learning and so that they are pro-actively engaging in upgrading the skills of their workforce and make them more competitive (Dar, Canagarajah and Murphy, 2003[37]).

Many OECD countries and partner countries and economies use levies systems, with vary levy rates (Box 4.3) and the size of employers' contributions varies significantly across countries, sectors, firm size or funds.

In Latin America, a good example of revenue-generating levy is Brazil's *S–system (Sistema-S)*. Training provided through S-system is financed by a 1-2.5% levy on enterprises' payroll that is collected by the social security system. Importantly, the Brazilian Ministry of Labour sets the training priorities that will set the goals of the training institutions supplying the training. The *S-system* covers different sectors going from industry and telecommunications (SENAI) to commerce (SENAC) and transport (SENAT). Moreover, there are specific institutes focussing on training for entrepreneurs and SMEs (SEBRAE, financed through several other funds), and for rural areas and social inclusion by providing literacy programmes (SENAR) (OECD, 2006[38]).

> **Box 4.3. Different designs and examples of training levies**
>
> The three major types of training levy schemes are i) revenue-generating (or revenue-raising) schemes, ii) levy-grant (or levy-rebate) schemes and iii) levy-exemption or train-or-pay schemes. However, in practice, countries often have hybrid schemes.
>
> - *Revenue-generating schemes*: Employers contributions are used to finance publicly provided training, such as vocational schools. This type of training levies therefore do very little to incentivise employers to provide training to the workforce. Small firms are usually exempt from paying this tax. A typical example of this scheme is the SENAI scheme in Brazil.
> - *Levy-grant schemes:* Levies are collected by training funds that focus on certain types of skills. Levy contributions are returned to firms that have to finance workers' training that meets the funds' criteria. The grant can sometimes even be larger than the levy paid. This creates an incentive for employers to provide training in pre-decided areas and skills. However, the disadvantage of this scheme is the high administrative costs for the firms, especially smaller ones. Examples of the schemes can be found across various OECD countries, notably France, Italy, Korea, the Netherlands and Poland.

- *Levy-exemption schemes*: Also known as cost-reimbursement schemes or "train-or-pay" schemes, under which a tax is imposed on employers, but which is reduced by the amount that enterprises spend on allowable training activities. This scheme has a lower administrative burden than the levy-grant scheme, but it assumes that firms know what their (and society's) training needs are. Moreover, it may subsidise training that employers would also have provided without the levy-exemption.

Although companies themselves pay the training levies, the real financial burden may fall on the employees, through lower net-of-tax wages. Who "really" pays for the training depends on how likely firms and workers are to adjust their behaviour based on changing training costs, and the bargaining power of different stakeholders such as trade unions. Moreover, another drawback of levies is that, in practice, large employers tend to benefit disproportionately from them. This is often because small firms lack the capacity to determine their training needs, to plan such training, and to file applications for cost reimbursement or grants. Examples of this scheme can be found in Australia, Belgium, Canada, Greece, Spain and the United Kingdom.

Source: OECD (2019[28]), *Getting Skills Right: Future-Ready Adult Learning Systems*, https://dx.doi.org/10.1787/9789264311756-en; OECD (2017[24]), *Financial Incentives for Steering Education and Training*, https://dx.doi.org/10.1787/9789264272415-en; Dar, A., S. Canagarajah and P. Murphy (2003[37]), *Training Levies: Rationale and Evidence from Evaluations*, http://documents.worldbank.org/curated/en/705121468779070378/Training-levies-evidence-from-evaluations.

References

Alaimo, V. et al. (2015), *Jobs for Growth*, Inter-American Development Bank, Washington, D.C., http://dx.doi.org/10.18235/0000139. [10]

Almeida, R., J. Behrman and D. Robalino (2012), *The Right Skills for the Job?: Rethinking Training Policies for Workers*, The World Bank, https://doi.org/10.1596/978-0-8213-8714-6. [23]

Bloom, N. and J. Van Reenen (2007), "Measuring and explaining management practices across firms and countries", *The Quarterly Journal of Economics*, Vol. 122/4, pp. 1351-1408. [29]

Bravo, J., A. García and H. Schlechter (2019), "Mercado Laboral Chileno para la Cuarta Revolución Industrial - Clapes UC", *Documentos de Trabajo*, No. 59, Clapes, Santiago de Chile, http://www.clapesuc.cl/investigaciones/doc-trabajo-no59-mercado-laboral-chileno-para-la-cuarta-revolucion-industrial/. [18]

Brown, C. et al. (2016), *Primer año del Programa + Capaz. Evidencia sobre Inserción laboral de Egresados*, Unidad de Estudios, Subsecretaría del Trabajo, Ministerio del Trabajo y Previsión Social, Gobierno de Chile. [19]

Busso, M. et al. (2017), *Learning Better: Public Policy for Skills Development*, Inter-American Development Bank, Washington, D.C, http://dx.doi.org/10.18235/0000799. [3]

Comisión Nacional de Productividad (2018), "Formación de Competencias para el Trabajo en Chile", Comisión Nacional de Productividad, Santiago de Chile, https://www.comisiondeproductividad.cl/estudios/formacion-de-competencias-para-el-trabajo-en-chile/. [17]

Crespi, G., E. Fernández-Arias and E. Stein (2014), *¿Cómo repensar el desarrollo productivo? Políticas e instituciones sólidas para la transformación económica.*. [12]

Dar, A., S. Canagarajah and P. Murphy (2003), *Training Levies: Rationale and Evidence from Evaluations*, World Bank, Washington D.C., http://documents.worldbank.org/curated/en/705121468779070378/Training-levies-evidence-from-evaluations. [37]

Ellis, S. (2003), "Anticipating employers' skills needs: The case for intervention", *International Journal of Manpower*, Vol. 24/1, pp. 83-96, http://dx.doi.org/10.1108/01437720310464981. [33]

Flores Lima, J., C. González-Velosa and D. Rosas-Shady (2014), *Cinco hechos: Sobre la capacitación en firma en America Latina y el Caribe*, Inter-American Development Bank, Washington, D.C. [25]

González-Velosa C., Rosas D. and Flores R. (2016), "On-the-job training in Latin America and the Caribbean: Recent evidence", in Grazzi M., P. (ed.), *Firm Innovation and Productivity in Latin America and the Caribbean*, Palgrave Macmillan, New York. [11]

Hunneus, C., C. de Mendoza and G. Rucci (2011), "El estado del arte de la capacitación de los trabajadores en América Latina and el Caribe", *Technical Note*, No. 346, Inter-American Development Bank, Washington, DC. [13]

Ibarrarán, P. and D. Rosas-Shady (2009), "Evaluating the impact of job training programmes in Latin America: Evidence from IDB funded operations", *Journal of Development Effectiveness*, Vol. 1/2, pp. 195-216. [9]

ILO (2016), *What Works: Active Labour Market Policies in Latin America and the Caribbean*, International Labour Organization, https://www.ilo.org/wcmsp5/groups/public/---dgreports/---dcomm/---publ/documents/publication/wcms_492373.pdf. [5]

Jaramillo, M., J. Baanante and T. Sanz (2009), *Evaluación independiente programa Construyendo Perú – Informe final*, Ministerio de Economía y Finanzas, Lima. [8]

Kaufmann, D., A. Kraay and P. Zoido-Lobaton (1999), "Governance matters", *Policy Research Working Paper*, No. WPS 2196, The World Bank, Washington, DC, http://documents.worldbank.org/curated/en/665731468739470954/Governance-matters. [4]

Larrañaga, O. et al. (2011), *Informe Final. Comisión Revisora Del Sistema de Capacitación e Intermediación Laboral*, Ministerio del Trabajo y Previsión Social, Santiago, https://www.undp.org/content/dam/chile/docs/pobreza/undp_cl_pobreza_InformeFinal_211011_doc2.pdf. [15]

Macroconsult S.A. (2012), *Evaluación de impacto del programa Construyendo Perú*, Unidad de Coordinación de Préstamos Sectoriales (UCPS), Ministerio de Economía y Finanzas. [7]

OECD (2019), *Getting Skills Right: Future-Ready Adult Learning Systems*, Getting Skills Right, OECD Publishing, Paris, https://dx.doi.org/10.1787/9789264311756-en. [28]

OECD (2019), *Getting Skills Right: Making Adult Learning Work in Social Partnership*, http://www.oecd.org/employment/emp/adult-learning-work-in-social-partnership-2019.pdf. [34]

OECD (2019), *OECD Economic Surveys: Colombia 2019*, OECD Publishing, Paris, https://dx.doi.org/10.1787/e4c64889-en. [2]

OECD (2019), *OECD Skills Strategy 2019: Skills to Shape a Better Future*, OECD Publishing, Paris, https://dx.doi.org/10.1787/9789264313835-en. [31]

OECD (2019), *Priorities for Adult Learning dashboard*, http://www.oecd.org/employment/skills-and-work/adult-learning/dashboard.htm. [27]

OECD (2019), "Public expenditure and participant stocks related to active labour market policies", *OECD.Stat (database)*, https://stats.oecd.org/Index.aspx?DataSetCode=LMPEXP (accessed on 11 December 2019). [6]

OECD (2018), *Getting Skills Right: Australia*, Getting Skills Right, OECD Publishing, Paris, https://dx.doi.org/10.1787/9789264303539-en. [35]

OECD (2018), *Getting Skills Right: Brazil*, Getting Skills Right, OECD Publishing, Paris, https://dx.doi.org/10.1787/9789264309838-en. [1]

OECD (2018), *OECD Economic Surveys: Chile 2018*, OECD Publishing, Paris, https://dx.doi.org/10.1787/eco_surveys-chl-2018-en. [14]

OECD (2017), *Financial Incentives for Steering Education and Training*, Getting Skills Right, OECD Publishing, Paris, https://dx.doi.org/10.1787/9789264272415-en. [24]

OECD (2017), *Survey of Adults Skills (PIAAC) (2012, 2015, 2017)*, (database), http://www.oecd.org/skills/piaac/. [21]

OECD (2016), *Getting Skills Right: Assessing and Anticipating Changing Skill Needs*, Getting Skills Right, OECD Publishing, Paris, https://dx.doi.org/10.1787/9789264252073-en. [22]

OECD (2006), *OECD Economic Surveys: Brazil 2006*, OECD Publishing, Paris, https://dx.doi.org/10.1787/eco_surveys-bra-2006-en. [38]

OECD/CAF/UN ECLAC (2016), *Latin American Economic Outlook 2017: Youth, Skills and Entrepreneurship*, OECD Publishing, Paris, https://dx.doi.org/10.1787/leo-2017-en. [39]

OECD/IDB (2016), *Broadband Policies for Latin America and the Caribbean: A Digital Economy Toolkit*, OECD Publishing, Paris, https://dx.doi.org/10.1787/9789264251823-en. [20]

OECD/ILO (2017), *Better Use of Skills in the Workplace: Why It Matters for Productivity and Local Jobs*, OECD Publishing, Paris, https://dx.doi.org/10.1787/9789264281394-en. [32]

Rodriguez, J. and S. Urzúa (2011), *An Evaluation of Training Programs Financed by Public Funds in Chile*, mimeo. [16]

The World Bank (2009), *The World Bank Enterprise Survey 2009-2017*, https://microdata.worldbank.org/index.php/catalog/enterprise_surveys. [26]

UNESCO (2018), *Funding Skills Development: The Private Sector Contribution*, UNESCO, Paris, https://unesdoc.unesco.org/ark:/48223/pf0000261984. [36]

World Management Survey (2015), *World Management Survey 2015*, https://worldmanagementsurvey.org. [30]

Notes

¹ ALMPs play a key role in helping unemployed finding jobs in developed OECD countries, however, in Latin America skills development programmes for unemployed are less prevalent.

² These results are based on the Survey on Productivity and Human Resources Training in Establishments (*Encuesta de Productividad y Formación de Recursos Humanos en Establecimientos* - EPFE), collected between 2011 and 2013. In every country except Colombia, surveys were representative at the national level. In Colombia, sampling was designed to make the survey representative at the sectoral level for three specific sectors: manufacturing, commerce, and services. Results presented in (González-Velosa C., Rosas D. and Flores R., 2016[11]) refer to the manufacturing sector.

³ Examples include the National University's Informatics Assistance and Training Institute (ICAI), the National Technical University's Centre for Communication and Information Technologies (CETICS)1 and Costa Rica University's Integral Programme for the Elderly.

⁴ www.sems.gob.mx/en_mx/sems/programa_circuito_conectados_contigo.

⁵ http://ovi.mt.gob.do/empleateya/home/.

⁶ The available data generally come from small-scale international surveys that may not be very representative of the varied landscape of adult learning in Latin America.

⁷ In addition, these statistics refer only to formal firms and are susceptible to over-estimate overall training participation as informal employment is not here measured.

⁸ Notice, however, that large firms still contribute nearly 70% to the region's gross domestic product (GDP) (OECD/CAF/UN ECLAC, 2016[39]).

⁹ Despite their name, however, the ISFs are not forecasts but rather qualitative snapshots of current and future skill needs in the industry.